Amulets and Pendants in Ancient Maharashtra

Dedicated to

My Parents

and

Chunnu

Amulets and Pendants in Ancient Maharashtra (3rd c. BC to 3rd c. CE)

by

Jyotsna Maurya

D.K. Printworld (P) Ltd.
NEW DELHI - 110 015

Cataloging in Publication Data — DK

Maurya, Jyotsna, 1970 –
Amulets and pendants in ancient Maharashtra, 3rd c. BC to 3rd c. CE.
Includes bibliographical references (p.).
Includes index.

1. Amulets — India — Maharashtra — History. 2. Pendants (Jewelry) —India — Maharastra — History. 3. Jewelry — India — Maharashtra — History. 4. Maharashtra (India) — Antiquities. I. Title

ISBN 81-246-0158-5

First published in India in 2000

Published and printed by :
D.K. Printworld (P) Ltd.
Regd. office : *'Sri Kunj'*, F-52, Bali Nagar
New Delhi - 110015
Phone: (011) 545-3975, 546-6019; *Fax*: (011) 546-5926
E-Mail: dkprint@4mis.com

Preface

One of the lesser-known aspects of Archaeology is the importance of beads. Here I have dealt with Amulets and Pendants of Mauryan and Sātavāhana period from Maharashtra. As a student of Archaeology I owed it to the specimens from archaeological excavations.

The study of amulets and pendants is useful in a variety of ways. It is the visible expression of the evolved aesthetic sense of humanity through successive millennia. The cultural interpretation of pendants and amulets has been resolved into religious, medicinal, social, technological, economic, and various other aspects.

It has been my privilege to study under the guidance and direction of Prof. S. B. Deo. He initiated me in bead studies and more important I benefited from his immense knowledge.

Discussions with my friend Peter Francis, Director of Bead Research Center, Lake Placid, was extremely illuminating.

Mr. Susheel Mittal, director of D.K. Printworld kindly agreed to publish this work. It is a pleasure for me to record here my gratefulness to all of them.

Comments and suggestions from the readers are most welcome and would be incorporated in the next edition of this book.

April 13, 2000 **Jyotsna Maurya**

Acknowledgements

I AM grateful to Professor M. S. Mate, Dr. S. L. Gokhale, Dr. G. L. Badam and Dr. Sushma Deo who have taken keen interest in the progress of my work and have provided me encouragement and help.

I am also thankful to R.R. Shigavan and late Shri S.C. Purandare of Deccan College Library, for their friendly assistance.

To my friends I am thankful for their help and encouragement.

This study is based on the publications by the Archaeological Survey and by different universities for which grateful thanks are due.

Let me thank my Guru, late Professor S. B. Deo, with a deep sense of gratitude, who had entrusted me with this subject and constantly encouraged me to complete this work. He was extremely cordial and helpful in the course of my work.

Special thanks to Dr. Vinod Sharma of Indira Gandhi Institute of Development and Research for his suggestion to publish this work.

Last but not least important is the patient support of my family members. I don't have adequate words to thank them.

April 13, 2000 **Jyotsna Maurya**

Abbreviations

AB	*Art Bulletin.*
ABIHI	*Annual Bibliography of Indian History and Indology.*
AI	*Ancient India*, New Delhi.
ARADGS	*Annual Report of the Archaeological Department of Gwalior State*, Bhopal.
ARADND	*Annual Reports of the Archaeological Department of H. E. H. the Nizam's Dominions*, Calcutta.
ARASI	*Annual Report of the Archaeological Survey of India*, Delhi.
ASI	*Archaeological Survey of India Reports* (published under the supervision of Sir Alexander Cunningham), Varanasi.
BBMFA	*Bulletin of the Museum of Fine Arts*, Boston.
BDCRI	*Bulletin of the Deccan College Post-Graduate and Research Institute*, Pune.
BIS	*Bharatiya Itihasa Ani Samskriti* (Marathi), Bombay.
BMGM	*Bulletin of the Madras Government Museum.*
BMPG	*Bulletin of Museum and Picture Gallery*, Baroda.
BPWM	*Bulletin of the Prince of Wales Museum*, Bombay.
HAS	*Hyderabad Archaeological Series*, Calcutta.
HOS	*Harvard Oriental Series.*
IAR	*Indian Archaeology: A Review*, New Delhi.

IHQ	*Indian Historical Quarterly*, Calcutta.
JAOS	*Journal of the American Oriental Society*, U.S.A.
JAS	*Journal of Asiatic Society*, Calcutta.
JBBRAS	*Journal of the Bombay Branch of the Royal Asiatic Society*, Bombay.
JGRS	*Journal of Gujarat Research Society*, Bombay.
JISOA	*Journal of the Indian Society of Oriental Art*, Calcutta.
JOI	*Journal of the Oriental Institute*, Baroda.
LK	*Lalit Kala*, Prince of Wales Museum, Mumbai.
MASI	*Memoirs of the Archaeological Survey of India*, Delhi.
SBE	*Sacred Books of the East*, Delhi, Varanasi, Patna.

List of Maps and Figures

Figure 3

Figure 4

Figure 5 — Bull Amulets

Figure 6

Figure 7

Figure 8

Figure 9 — Cylindrical Amulets

Figure 10 — Sculptural Parallels

Figure 11 — Sculptural Parallels

Figure 12 — Sculptural Parallels

1

Cultural and Historical Importance of Amulets and Pendants

AMULETS and pendants have been worn by men and women on their persons set within necklaces, girdles, bracelets and anklets. In general, they were used mostly in necklaces. It is possible that they have been used individually for various reasons. It is more so in the case of amulets. A pendant is a hanging jewel, or a member of ornament, especially one attached to a necklace, bracelet, etc.

Pendants are of simple and conventional shapes generally without any special importance. On the contrary, amulets have been found to possess definite shapes, so designed for some magico-religious or superstitious reasons. In some cases, it is rather difficult to assert whether a particular pendant has an amuletic value or was used for aesthetic convenience. An amulet is defined in the *Oxford English Dictionary* as anything worn on the person as a charm or as preventive against evil, mischief, disease, witchcraft, etc., its derivation is the latin word, *Amuletum*.

According to Sir. C.A. Wallis Budge (180) the Egyptologist, an amulet exercises its protective powers continuously and in general over its owner. Pliny uses the word 'amulet' to describe an object, which preserves a man from some trouble; medical or prophylactic treatments; and a substance used in medicine.

Seligmann (1920: 26) is of the opinion that an 'Amulet' is a means of defense. Amulet is an object, which is endowed with magical powers. Amulet of its own accord uses these powers ceaselessly on behalf of the person who carries it. Or causes it to be laid up in his house, or attaches it to someone of his possessions, to protect him and his belongings from the attacks of evil spirits or from the Evil Eye.

Amulet is a material object worn generally around the neck by a person for some magico-religious reasons, for example, to cure disease, to give strength, 'luck' or general protection to the possessor or to defend him or her from specific danger or misfortunes.

Amulet is made to bestow on the wearer long life, safety from disease and demons, protection from the attacks of sorcerers, and enemies. So the amulet naturally possessed some power and the ceremony of wearing it and the supposed spell rendered it superhuman. In order to be clear and also to emphasise their importance, both of them are dealt with separately in the fifth chapter.

The use of the amulets and pendants was not confined to any one place or period. They are traced in ornaments, almost all over the world, from a very early age. The great mass of the evidence about these now available justifies the statement that the use of amulets was, and still is, universal.

The amulets worn by primitive men and women were made of simple natural substances. At first they were of unusual form and/or distinct colour. Sometimes they were worn because the material was new to them. The oldest amulets were such objects or material, which roused man's curiosity, or excited his wonder and admiration. His natural love of possession led him to make these his property.

Stones of unusual colours or having markings on them or with veins of different colours running through them, were promptly taken possession of by him. He especially prised a stone, which had natural perforation. The credit of having introduced the wearing of amulets in the world belongs to the first man who threaded such a stone on a thong cut from the skin of some animal, and then hung it round his neck. The perforated stone suggested to him the boring of other stones which he used as amulets and which he could then hang on his body. We shall never know fully what primitive man expected his various amulets to do for him, or how he thought they worked for his good. Similarly, what meaning was attached to the word 'amulet' by its inventors, or by those who first used one shall remain obscure.

Human belief in magical symbols contained in geometric or other designs is a very old one. In course of time, these designs came to be incorporated probably in portable charms and amulets, so that the potent in them could be easily carried on persons. This gave rise to their coming into jewellery and forming part of it. Most of these designs are associated with some common belief, magic or religious ideas and many have deeply significant meanings. It is clear that the people of different periods and cultures always believed in the superhuman potential of some stones to ward off the evil effects of various planets and diseases. These stones also conferred health, wealth, fame, fortune and longevity on the possessor. It is again quite clear from the number and variety of these that there was no single amulet, which was believed to be capable of protecting man from every danger.

The subject has received very scanty attention in India. Accurately dated specimens are comparatively few and are inadequately published. The subject has three main aspects: (i) archaeological; (ii) techno-cultural and typological study of dated specimens; and lastly (iii) references to the use of amulets in Indian literature and sculpture and its concordance with the archaeological data. Unless these are marshalled fully no accurate picture of the use of amulets or pendants in India can be obtained.

In India, amulets, pendants and beads are recovered from Paleolithic to mediaeval culture sites. However, the history of amulets and pendants in ancient India has not been studied fully. A few attempts have been made on different lines. To list a few these are Deo, Dikshit, Margabandhu, Francis and Niharika.

Amulets and pendants have a very early history in India. Their origin can be traced as far back as the Chalcolithic period and Vedic times. A book devoted to magical charms like the *Atharvaveda* (Whitney: 1905), naturally contains numerous references to different kinds of amulets and their properties. In this period the amulets were chosen from every sort of material from vegetable kingdom, animal kingdom, minerals, manufactured objects, etc. The amulets were made of various materials, like wood, herb, shell, gold, pearl, etc. These amulets are largely derived from the vegetable kingdom, the designation of the plant being generally quite obscure. Good examples of the symbolic treatment are offered by the charm to cure. Universally speaking, hair, teeth, claws, shells, coral, animals and stone products also have a place in the list of amulets and charms. The *Atharvaveda* has abundantly referred to the amulets supposed to secure the immediate fulfilment of each and every desire. The word for amulet in the *Atharvaveda* is *maṇi*. Some of the charms of the *Atharvaveda* are meant to accompany the rituals wherein an amulet plays an important part. The amulet naturally possessed some power and the ceremony and spell rendered it superhuman. The hymns themselves now and then recount the achievement of tasks due to use of an amulet.

In the Atharvavedic times, amulets were widely used for a large variety of purposes. But it is the *Atharvaveda* that has abundantly employed the amulet to secure the immediate fulfilment of each and every desire. In fact, there was hardly any trouble, which the amulets and spells could not cure or avert. Hence, the whole of the *Atharvaveda* is teeming with spells addressed to or invoking amulets.

They were worn by the ill round the necks or arms. They were made effective by uttering of charms. They were both offensive and defensive. They drove away and protected the wearer from demons. They brought prosperity and expelled poverty. They gave long life to the wearers and cured them of all diseases. They frustrated the hostile charms of the sorcerers.

The Atharvavedic poets gave them a respectable ancestry by regarding them as known to the gods and brāhmaṇas of yore. The *Gṛhya-sūtra*s mention them in a considerable portion. The most tangible evidence of these amulets is available from objects of various descriptions obtained from the excavations of various ancient sites in India and surface picking, and housed in various museums.

For an in-depth study the author restricts herself to the specimens recovered from Maharashtra. In case of data from Maharashtra, these studies must also be supplemented with various aspects of the problem such as contacts with other regions in India, which were responsible for the occurrence of different shapes in different periods.

The present study surveys all the data pertaining to the three aspects mentioned above. In archaeological record we find the use of beads from the Upper Paleolithic times. Amulets and pendants were commonly used in the Neolithic cultures and their use was followed in the successive Chalcolithic, Megalithic and early historic period. These are in use even today.

In Maharashtra, such amulets are found to have been worn from as early as the Chalcolithic age. During the early historical period quite a variety of amulets and pendants were in vogue. A large number of them have been reported from excavated sites in Maharashtra datable to *circa* the third century BCE to the third century CE.

The study of amulets and pendants is useful in a variety of ways. It is the visible expression of the evolved aesthetic sense of humanity through successive millennia.

The social importance of amulets and pendants

Amulets and pendants also help to interpret certain aspects of social life in the past. This is true of societies not only in India but also elsewhere. In India, such an interpretation gains an enhanced tempo owing to the corroborative evidences met within ancient literature and sculpture as for instance, *triratna* amulet.

Thus, the archaeological and the literary evidences open a vast field for understanding the role of amulets in the cultural life of the Indians.

Material used for pendants may also indicate the social status of the user. Only affluent people could import the non-indigenous material from distant lands.

Certain types of beads seem to have been made of common materials of a cheaper variety such as terracotta, and copied after the specimens made of relatively expensive material. Terracotta specimens may be regarded as the poor man's possessions and therefore have great value as sources of social and religious history. It is usual for the poor classes to imitate the fashions of the rich within their standards. This can also point to higher demand of the type as it is possible to produce it on large scale in a short span of time.

The rarity of a pendant found in the course of limited excavation may not enable one to give a complete picture of the lifestyle in a particular period but it indicates its use by a certain class whose demands were above the levels of an ordinary artist. It is such special type that enables us to know more of the technological expertise of the times. Such pendants give us inkling into the class structure of the then society.

Their material also indicates the social status of the users, as for instance, certain non-indigenous materials.

The religious importance of amulets and pendants

The religious significance of certain amulets and pendants is evident in many cases. Religious symbols have played no insignificant part in the shaping of certain pendants and their cultural importance needs no emphasis. Several symbols show the magnitude of the hold which religion had on contemporary society. This is clear in Buddhist context, for example, the casket amulet from Paunār in crystal.

A man carried the claws and teeth, of lions and tigers and

other savage and powerful animals because he believed they would add to his strength in fighting wild beasts and human foes.

The economic importance of amulets and pendants

The study of such may provide an insight into the progress of lapidary art in a particular period. It must be realised that the painstaking minute work done by the craftsman and the creation of the various forms by the artists is no mean work. It was a craft of great skill and was confined to a special class of workers, as is today. The process of making amulets and pendants involves division of labour and specialisation in the various stages of manufacture, for a single artisan could not work through all the stages in its making, such as bringing the material, shaping rough-outs, cutting, polishing, drilling, etc.

The art of valuing precious stones and gems was a difficult science and was respected accordingly.

Some of the amulets and pendants have dating value as the manufacture and use of some special shape of amulets was confined to a particular period, for example, spacer pendants seem to have been popular in the Sātavāhana period.

Certain medicinal properties are attached to amulets, which were supposed to cure some ailments, sometimes they were used also as charms.

Close resemblance of amulet and pendants and their typology from many sites in northern and southern India demonstrates that cultural intercourse was common between these regions.

The materials, which are not indigenous to India like, lapis-lazuli, being mostly found in Afghanistan, must have reached some sites by way of trade. It is not only the cultural influence infiltrating the country from outside which forms useful basis for the study of amulets and pendants, but within the country itself the trade-routes and the geographical peculiarities go a long way in establishing the widespread distribution of certain types of amulets and pendants.

The abundance of a material might indicate — as for instance, agate and carnelian — the proximity of the source of and the possibility of a local industry working on it. Paucity, on the other hand, might indicate the difficulty in obtaining the material, the higher cost of production and the restricted use of the material by only the affluent classes.

On the other hand, it is also possible to surmise that the material was not much favoured or was perhaps out of fashion.

The cultural importance of amulets and pendants

The cultural interpretation of pendants and amulets can be resolved into religious, medicinal, social, technological, economic and various other aspects.

The study of forms and ornamentation of amulets and pendants of a particular period discloses man's curious fascination for the unusual, the rare, the shining, the colourful metals, stones and other materials. It also helps us to understand the belief, the customs, the economic conditions, and the set-up of the society. Thus, such a study opens up the book of life.

It is evident that the study of amulets and pendants, is not only a study of the superficial tendencies of luxurious habits of man, but is important in understanding the development of successive stages of change in shape, if any.

Why certain objects were chosen as amulets is quite clear in some cases, but in others we can only make a guess.

Inferences regarding foreign cultural and/or trade contacts can in many instances, be drawn from the study of the materials from which the amulets and pendants were made.

So amulets go a long way in establishing certain decorative or religious norms in a particular geographical region. Such amulets were possibly carried by travellers to wider and distant regions and thus throw an interesting side light on typological migration and contact.

2

The Technological Importance of Amulets and Pendants

AFTER having studied the cultural and historical importance of amulets and pendants in the life of people it will be fruitful to study the technical aspects also. In recent years researches have been carried out regarding the techniques of making amulets and pendants. The archaeological data provides sufficient information regarding the various techniques in the making of beads. Here the process is summarised with the help of examples recovered from Maharashtra.

Perforation

Perforating a bead was a very important stage in completing the process of manufacture. Obviously it depended on the material of which the pendant and amulet was made.

The technique and the process of perforation were related to harder materials like stone or softer material like talc or material used in moulding a bead as of terracotta. Apart from this, the nature of use of the pendant, as also its position in the necklace (for instance spacer) was also taken into consideration before perforating the specimen.

The main types of perforation in stone were five:

1. Single perforation.
2. Double perforation.
3. 'L' shape perforation.
4. 'T' shape perforation.
5. 'Y and V' shape perforation or Miscellaneous.

The former involved boring the specimen from one end. This could be possible in small, short beads, only; otherwise this resulted in the breakage in case of a long bead because of wider thrust of the drill in the core of the bead (*fig*. 1.3).

The second type of perforation was 'double perforation', i.e., drilling from both the ends (*fig*. 1.5). This resulted in an hourglass like section. The skill lay in adjusting the points of drill from both ends in such a way as to make them meet generally in the centre of the inner core of the bead (*fig*. 1.1). Specimens are, however, known from several sites wherein the drilling has been not that precise, resulting in different lengths of the boring or, if done immaturely, with perforations not meeting (*fig*. 1.2).

The third and rather infrequent type of perforation is the 'L-shaped' one. Here the perforations formed a right angle. Such a perforation was executed in view of the placement of the specimen in a necklace (*fig*. 1.10).

Yet another variety was of 'V-shaped' perforation which helped to separate the strands in a necklace (*fig*. 1.6). The spacers, obviously, had more than one perforation with a view to keep the strands in position (*figs*. 1.7 & 1.8). The technique of perforating moulded specimens (in terracotta, faience, talc, etc.) was obviously simple (*fig*. 1.4).

When a bead was used as the central piece it had 'T-shaped perforation (*fig*. 1.9).

It is possible to quote specimens of the above varieties of perforations from the excavated data in Maharashtra.

Perforation was sometimes done from both the sides, for example, a natural nodule from Nevāsā (*fig*. 4.3) is neatly perforated from both sides which has resulted in a perforation of hourglass section.

In 'L' shape perforation, perforation from two sides is evident (*fig*. 2.1). A small cavity or depression seems to have been made for steadying the drill in the specimen and is a feature very commonly noticed amongst pendants of all material.

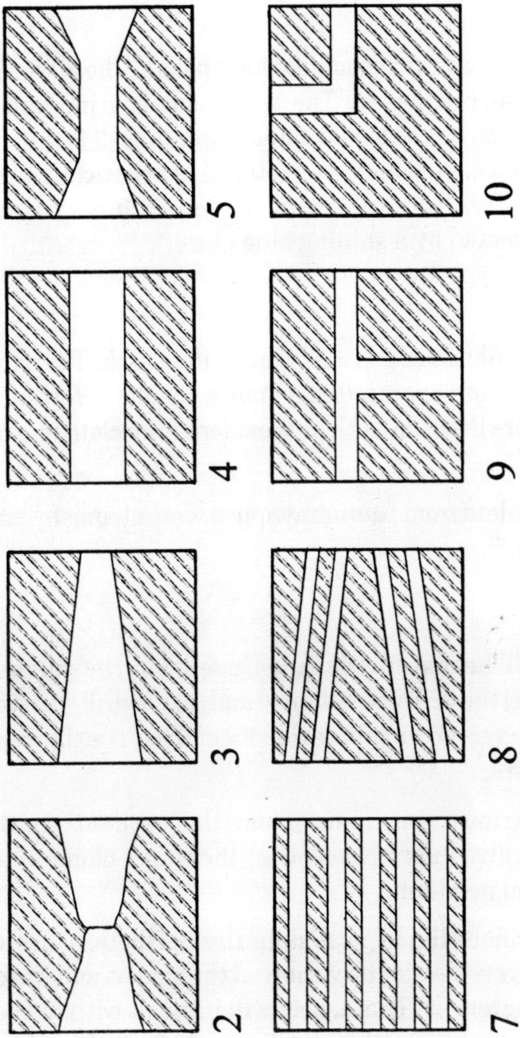

FIGURE - 1.

Polish

Some of the amulets and pendants bear polish. These were made smooth and then polished. The specimens bearing polish are from Nāsik (*figs*. 2.6, 4.1) and Bhokardan (*figs*. 2.9, 4.6). These are very well polished and the material is artistically selected. Bhokardan (*fig*. 7.3) specimen seems to have been very dexterously coated by a shining blue glaze.

Mould

Terracotta amulets are generally made in moulds. For example, Nandī amulets are executed in a double mould. A few moulded specimens were dried on cloth as is evident from cloth impression on them.

Shell amulets from Kauṇḍinyapura were strung by rubbing the cones (*fig*. 7.9).

Drills

Two types of bronze drills were used for the purpose of perforation: (1) the drill with a flange and (2) the drill with twisted grooves. However, no tangible evidence of these is so far reported in Maharashtra.

Thus, various specimens from the excavated sites in Maharashtra give information about the stages of manufacture of amulets and pendants.

Besides this technological skill, the aesthetic sense of the people is also revealed in the variety of the shapes and the choice of different materials. This aspect will be dealt with in the fifth chapter. After studying the significance which these amulets and pendants have, we shall now turn to the study of the excavated sites from which this data comes, in the third chapter.

So the study of amulets and pendants reveals different stages of technological development and limitations that particular period or community with which they are associated. These also point towards the division of labour and specialisation in that particular art.

3

Excavations in Maharashtra A Summary

AROUND the third-century BC cities flourished in Maharashtra after a Dark Age. This is evident from the cultural remains of the Mauryan and the Sātavāhana periods, which were investigated in the nineteenth and the twentieth centuries by Indian scholars.

Cities of this period were characterised by the use of iron and urban-life. Except Nevāsā rest of the excavations were vertical; so, we do not get enough information about the extent of the cities, and the economic, social and religious life of the inhabitants.

Excavations which have yielded cultural remains belonging to the Mauryan and the Sātavāhana periods are those at Brahmapurī, Karāḍ, Kauṇḍinyapura, Kolhāpur, Nāsik, Nevāsā, Paiṭhan, Paunār, Paunī, Prakāshe, Sopārā and Ter (Map 1). The reports of most of these are published except of a few. A glance over the archaeological investigations carried out in respect of the Mauryan and the Sātavāhana sites in Maharashtra has given an insight into their material culture. However, the description will necessarily be sketchy in parts where no or very little information is available. It will be somewhat detailed in case of certain sites where the data is abundant. The sitewise data is as follows:

Adam (21° 00'N: 79° 27'E) is situated on the left bank of the Wāghor river of the Waingaṅgā drainage system, in Kuhi *tāluka* of Vidarbha region. This site is about 60 km SE of Nāgpur (*IAR*, 1988-9: 50-62).

Three trenches were taken by Amarendra Nath of the Excavations Branch of the ASI, Nāgpur, with the objective to ascertain —

(1) the cultural sequence and chronology of the site,

(2) its interrelationship with other contemporary cultures of the region,

(3) the nature and formation of the *stūpa*, the rampart and the moat, and

(4) to understand the settlement pattern within the rampart.

The excavation has revealed five cultural periods beginning with (1) Mesolithic and followed by (2) Neolithic, (3) Chalcolithic, (4) Mauryan and (5) Sātavāhana.

Four decorated ivory pendants and some copper ones, four hundred and eighty-six beads in agate, bone, carnelian, chalcedony, chert, copper, glass, ivory, terracotta, etc., were unearthed. Two multi-grooved sandstone slab fragments of bead-polishers and lead spools have been recovered, but their period is not mentioned.

Ārnī (20° 4'N: 78° 57'E) in Darwā *tāluka*, Yeotmāl district is situated on the left bank of the Aruṇāvatī river, a tributary of the Pengaṅgā, in Vidarbha. It provides extensive remains of ancient habitations. A.M. Shastri of Nāgpur University excavated this site for two seasons, 1978-9 and 1981-2 (*IAR*, 1978-9: 71-2; *IAR*, 1981-2: 55-6).

The excavation was conducted at the northern side of the habitational mound locally known as Pañca-Pāṇḍava Ṭekaḍī. The excavation uncovered three periods of occupations, beginning with (1) Megalithic and followed by (2) Mauryan and (3) Sātavāhana. These diggings were on small scale and therefore very little is known about the total personality of this site. A *triratna* amulet is reported from Sātavāhana period, which is noteworthy.

Bahāl (20° 35'N: 75° 5'E) in east Khāndesh is situated on the

Gīrṇā river. The site was excavated by M.N. Despande of South-Western Circle of the ASI (*IAR*, 1956-7: 17-18). This was done in continuation of the earlier trial excavation in 1952, which had established the Chalcolithic nature of its earliest level.

The excavation brought to light five periods, with breaks, beginning with (1) the Chalcolithic and followed by (2) the Mauryan and (3) the Sātavāhana. Beads of agate, carnelian and crystal were found in the Mauryan level. One appears to be a tooth pendant. After a long gap of twelve centuries, the site was re-occupied during the Yādava and the Muslim times.

Details about material typology of beads are lacking, as a full report has not been published.

Bhokardan (20° 16'N: 75° 46'E), ancient Bhogavardhana, is in the Auraṅgābād district of Marāṭhwāḍā region (Deo and Gupte 1973).

The ancient town of Bhogavardhana stood on the ancient trade route from Ujjain to Pratiṣṭhāna (Paiṭhan). It lies half way between Ajantā and Auraṅgābād.

Bhogavardhana is mentioned very frequently in early Brāhmī inscriptions. Bhogavardhana was an important centre of Brāhmaṇical worship as corroborated by a cave here which is assigned to the eighth century CE.

The history of Bhokardan in Kaḷacurī-Rāṣṭrakūṭa, Yādava and Khaljī periods is well-known from literary sources.

Excavations were undertaken by S.B. Deo and R.S. Gupte of Nāgpur and Marāṭhwāḍā universities respectively, to know the history and life of the people of ancient Bhogavardhana (*IAR*: 1972-3: 20-1; 1973-4: 20). It has revealed three periods beginning with (1) Mauryan and followed by (2) Sātavāhana and (3) post-Sātavāhana.

All the mounds at Bhogavardhana were found to have been extremely rich in the yield of beads. Not only the excavated trenches but surface explorations also gave a fairly rich collection of beads. In all, one thousand nine hundred and thirty-three beads were recovered. As many as eighteen different materials contributed to the make-up of Bhokardan beads. These are agate, amethyst, calcite, carnelian, chalcedony, coral, crystal, faience, garnet, glass, ivory, jade, jasper, lapis-lazuli, opal, shell and terracotta. The material wise distribution shows that terracotta contributed to the make-up of one-third of the collection. As compared to any other Sātavāhana site, Bhokardan has yielded a reasonably good amount of ivory beads.

In the Sātavāhana deposits, two soapstone moulds for beads have been found. The intact one has channels for lift-up. The two-halves, in both cases, could be joined later when in leather-hard condition. The nodules of crystal, carnelian and agate, unfinished beads and bead-mould in the deposit of this period of occupation indicate that like the shell bangle and ivory industry, Bhokardan also had a flourishing bead-making industry during the Sātavāhana and the post-Sātavāhana periods.

Brahmapurī (16° 41'N: 74° 71'E) is situated on the right bank of the Pañcagaṅgā river, in the western part of the city of Kolhāpur. From the inscriptional evidences and archaeological excavations, Kolhāpur appears to have flourished under the Sātavāhanas, the Śilāhāras, the Yādavas and the Marāṭhās.

The immediate cause of the excavation was the discovery of a bronze statuette of Poseidon, a bronze toy cart, etc., by K.G. Kundangar, Director of the State Archaeological Department, in trial digging on the site (Khandalwala 1960: 29-75).

Large-scale excavations were conducted by H. D. Sankalia and M.G. Dikshit, of Deccan College in 1945 (Sankalia and Dikshit 1952: 1-11; see also Gupta 1963: 38).

The excavation has revealed four cultural periods beginning with (1) the Sātavāhana, and followed by (2) the Late Sātavāhana, (3) the Bahmanī and (4) the Moghul.

Brahmapurī has yielded more than a thousand beads. The material of the beads comprises of agate, amethyst, carnelian, chalcedony, crystal, faience, garnet, glass, green jasper, gold, lapis-lazuli, seeds, shell, steatite, and terracotta.

Jorwe (19°33' N: 74°17'E) is situated on the left bank of the Pravarā river in Ahmadnagar district. The site, as the excavation showed, is a single culture — chalcolithic — site. There is no debris of later period (Sankalia and Deo 1955: 147-8).

Only one bead was found. It is of smoky chalcedony with long tubular shape and with the outer surface well polished.

Karāḍ (17°17'N: 74°13'E) is located on the junction of the rivers the Kr̥ṣṇā and the Koyanā, in Satārā district. This place was of considerable importance from a remote past and was esteemed with high sanctity (*BISM*, 1949: 1-3).

The earliest literary evidence for the antiquity of Karāḍ is from the *Mahābhārata*. Moreover, in the vicinity there are about 63 Buddhist caves assignable to the first half of the second century BC.

Karāḍ figures in old inscriptions as Karahāṭaka, which are dated to first-second century CE. In the sixth century, this came under the rule of the early Cāḷukyas of Bādāmī. In the tenth century CE the Rāṣṭrakūṭas and the Cāḷukyas of Trikaḷiṅga ruled here. They were succeeded by the Śilāhāras, later by the Cālukyas of Kalyāṇī, the Vijayanagara rulers, the Muslims and the Marāṭhās.

The Bhārata Itihāsa Saṁsodhaka Maṇḍal, Poona carried out explorations, in 1948 at Paṅtāchā Goṭ in Karāḍ. Karāḍ has yielded Sātavāhana remains.

Forty beads were found. These are made of the following materials: carnelian, crystal, glass, red jasper, shell and terracotta. One shell bead has the shape of a thunderbolt. It is flat on both sides and its edges have been cut with a very sharp instrument. It bears two holes along the horizontal axis and was perhaps used as a spacer. One of the terracotta beads has a rare shape, viz., that of a hubbed wheel.

Kauṇḍinyapura (20°55'N: 78° 05'E) in Chandur *tāluka* of Amarāvatī district is situated on the western bank of the Wardhā river. It is one of the few places, which retains its traditional name along with archaeological remains (Dikshit 1968: 1-7; *IAR*, 1961-2: 29-30). The antiquity of Vidarbha in which Kauṇḍinyapura is situated can be traced to the *Brāhmaṇas*, the Upaniṣads and the *Mahābhārata*. It appears amongst the countries subdued by the Sātavāhana ruler Vāsiṣṭhīputra Puḷumāvī. Copper-plates belonging to the Vākāṭakas, the Kalacuris, the Rāṣṭrakūṭas and the Yādavas of Devagirī give information about the region around Kauṇḍinyapura.

The *Bṛhat-saṁhitā* of Varāhamihira, *Vāsudevahiṇḍi*, *Thānāṅga Sutta*, *Nāyadhammakahāo* and the *Pañhāvāgaraṇa Ṭīkā* also allude to this place (see Dikshit 1968).

Vertical excavations were carried out by M.G. Dikshit (1968) of the Nāgpur University for two seasons in 1962-4.

The excavations revealed six periods of occupation, beginning with (1) Megalithic and followed by (2) Pre-Mauryan, (3) Mauryan, (4) Sātavāhana, (5) Late Sātavāhana and (6) Muslim.

In spite of the very limited extent of the excavation, the total yield of beads was quite high, being 395 in number. The period wise distribution of these was as follows: Megalithic — 54 beads in a necklace; Pre-Mauryan — 20; Mauryan — 103; Sātavāhana — 105; Late Sātavāhana —17; and Muslim — 14 beads.

A small-scale industry for the manufacture of beads existed at the site during the Sātavāhana period as evidenced by several unperforated specimens.

The material of the beads comprises of semi-precious stones like agate, amethyst, carnelian, chalcedony, crystal, garnet, jasper, lapis-lazuli, quartz, steatite, and materials like glass, shell and terracotta. Copper is used scarcely. Glass seems to have been introduced during the Mauryan period.

Nāsik (20° N: 73° 51'E) is an ancient town situated on both the banks of the Godāvarī (Sankalia and Deo 1955: 1-9).

Literary, epigraphical and monumental evidence supplies almost an unbroken history of Nāsik for nearly 2,500 years.

This pre-eminent position it held probably because it lay on the best route between central India and the West Coast.

The earliest well-authenticated mention of Nāsik is by Patañjali who flourished in *c.* 150 BC. This town in the Deccan was known to several writers like Varāhamihira (CE 550), and the authors of the *Vāyu* and the *Varāha* Purāṇas, *Atharvavedapariśiṣṭa*, *Āvaśyakacūrṇī* and *Nandīsūtra*. Between 200 BC-CE 300, Sātavāhanas, Śakas and Ahīras governed this region. It was definitely under the territories of the Traikūṭakas, the Kaḷacurīs, the Western Cāḷukyas, the Rāṣṭrakūṭas, the Muslims and finally the Marāṭhās.

H. D. Sankalia of Deccan College Post-Graduate and Research Institute carried out vertical excavations, in 1950-1.

The excavation revealed seven periods of occupation beginning with (1) Chalcolithic, and followed by (2) Early historic, (3) Sātavāhana, (4) Indo-Roman, (5) Early Muslim, (6) Moghul and (7) Marāṭhā.

Total yield of beads was 170. The material of beads comprises of agate, amethyst, bloodstone, bone, carnelian, crystal, glass, gold, jasper, lapis lazuli, opal, quartz, shell, soapstone and terracotta. Out of the, total yield, 53 per cent are made of terracotta.

The absence of unfinished beads shows that Nāsik was not a bead industry site at any time. A minute differentiation in the arecanut shape is found at Nāsik like that at Kośam.

The shapes of the carnelian beads of Nāsik are common and the single-etched bead (Sankalia and Deo 1955: fig. 45.18; Beck 1941: Pl. II.21) is exactly similar to the one found at Taxilā. The dates of both these tally well. Besides this, the absence of unfinished beads or large cores of these stones at Nāsik also point towards trade-contacts. Two lapis-lazuli beads have been found. This material is not indigenous to India. It is therefore, likely that these came to Nāsik from outside.

Along with tabular-triangular shapes and drop pendant, two peculiar pendants found in Period II are outstanding for shape and polish. One has a hexagonal body with two caps and two others are lion-shaped pendants.

Nevāsā (19°31'N: 75°E) in Ahmednagar district is situated on the Pravarā, a major tributary of the Godāvarī. The town of Nevāsā is located on both the banks of the river.

Traditional accounts regarding Nevāsā are very few. A section called Mahālaya Māhātmya in the *Skanda Purāṇa* tries to explain the name as originating from Nidhivāsa. The earliest literary references to Nevāsā are found in *Līḷācaritra* and some manuscripts of the Jñāneśvarī. Nevāsā is again mentioned as Nidhivāsa in *Ratnamālāstrotra* of Kesirāyā Vyāsa.

Inscriptional reference to Nevāsā is so for only one. This is in a record of Yādava Rāmacandra of 1278 CE. Explorations of Chalcolithic sites in the Godāvarī-Pravarā valley was undertaken and thus Nevāsā and other sites were brought to light (Sankalia *et. al.* 1960: 1-13; *IAR*, 1959-60: 25-8).

H.D. Sankalia carried out a horizontal excavation in 1954-6 on the Lāḍmoḍ mound. The main periods at the site and its neighbourhood are the following: (1) Early Paleolithic, (2) Middle Paleolithic, (3) Chalcolithic, (4) Early Historical, (5) Indo-Roman, (6) Muslim and (7) Marāṭhā.

Nevāsā has yielded one thousand six hundred and fifty-five beads. Periods 4 and 5 yielded about two-thirds of the total quantity. Steatite was the most favourite material of the Chalcolithic period (3), while faience, glass and terracotta were extensively used for bead-making in the Indo-Roman period (*IAR*, 1955-6: 8-11; 1959-60: 25-8).

Incomplete specimens indicate local manufacture of beads. As glass beads were found along with scores of pieces of glass slag, it becomes certain that Nevāsā was a glass bead-making and bangle-producing site at least in the Indo-Roman, Muslim and Marāṭhā periods.

Paiṭhan (19°28'N: 75° 24'E) is situated on a meander of the Godāvarī river, in Auraṅgābād district (*ASIAR WI*, 1876 IIIrd Vol.).

Paiṭhan, famous in ancient Indian literature as Pratiṣṭhāna, a town of self-importance, is referred to in Jaina, Buddhist and Brāhmaṇical literature. The Jaina literature especially, and more so the *Bṛhat-Kalpasūtra-Bhāṣya*, associates it with the Sātavāhanas and the Nāgas. Periplus of the Erythrean Sea and Ptolemy also refer to it. During the Sātavāhana rule, it was the capital town connected by trade route to Bharoch in the NW, Nāneghāṭ in the West and Ter in the SE. In the Yādava period it seems to have developed as a sacred place.

In spite of its long history and apart from the legends and the myths associated with it, Paiṭhan has not been systematically excavated on a large-scale. In 1936-7, G. Yazadani, of the Archaeological Department of Nizam's Dominion, excavated at Paiṭhan. But full details of the dig were not adequately published (Syed Yusuf 1936: 39-42).

M.G. Dikshit, of the Department of Archives, Maharashtra State, conducted some trial excavations at Kausan near Paiṭhan. The full report of this excavation is not yet published (*IAR*, 1965-6: 28-9).

This excavation has yielded a four-fold cultural sequence beginning with (1) Mauryan, and followed by (2) Sātavāhana and Late Sātavāhana, (3) Rāṣṭrakūṭa and (4) Muslim-Marāṭhā.

The Sātavāhana period finds include glass beads with lug-collars, cobalt-coloured melon or gadrooned beads, and terracotta bullae in imitation of Roman coins.

Paunār (20°47' N: 78°41'E) in *tāluka* and district Wardhā, is situated on the right bank of the river Dham, a tributary of the Wardhā (Deo and Dhavalikar 1968: 1-7; *IAR*, 1966-7: 27).

Paunār has been identified with ancient Pravarapura, the capital of the Vākāṭakas who ruled over Vidarbha, from the third to the sixth century CE. About the beginning of the Christian era, this region, no doubt, formed part of the Sātavāhana Empire. In the third century BC Paunār, along with other parts of Vidarbha, was included in the Aśokan Empire as is eloquently borne out by the existence of a fragmentary inscription of the famous emperor at Deoṭak.

S.B. Deo of Nāgpur University carried vertical excavations out here on the Quillā mound in 1967. The excavations have shown that the antiquity of Paunār can be stretched back to at least the beginning of the first millennium BC.

The excavation has unearthed four cultural periods beginning with the (1) Chalcolithic and followed by (2) Sātavāhana, (3) Vākāṭaka, (4) Viṣṇukuṇḍin, (5) Kaḷacurī and (6) Muslim.

One hundred and seventeen beads representing thirteen materials like agate, calcite, carnelian, chalcedony, coral, crystal, garnet, glass, jasper, lapis-lazuli, marble, shell and terracotta were collected during the excavation. These show the use of mostly local material except coral, marble and lapis-lazuli.

The distribution of beads show that no bead could be had from Period 1. The bead-making activity seems to have increased in the subsequent periods, the largest collection belonging to the horizons of Period 3, which was the period of maximum prosperity in the history of Paunār. There is a decline, not only in the number of beads but in the range of materials used for beads, in the subsequent period.

Paunī (79°39'N: 20°48'E) in Bhaṅḍārā district is about three km SE of Wainagaṅgā, one of the most sacred rivers of the Vidarbha region. It has a perennial flow.

H. Cousens noticed Paunī as an ancient fort in 1897. Marshall, Hargreaves, Cunningham, have also referred to the fortifications at Paunī. In 1935, a stone inscription was discovered at Paunī belonging to the Bhāraśivas. Later, in 1964, a pillar inscription of Mahākṣatrapa Rupiammā was noticed who belonged to the Śaka race. Mauryas, Śuṅgas, Sātavāhanas and Kṣatrapas ruled over this region. In the post-Sātavāhana period,

Vidarbha passed under the Vākāṭakas.

S.B. Deo and J.P. Joshi carried out vertical excavations. The excavations were spread over two working seasons 1969-70 on the Jaggannātha Ṭekaḍī, Chandakapūra Ṭekaḍī and Hardolāla Ṭekaḍī (*IAR*, 1968-9: 14-16; 1969-70: 20-1).

The excavations revealed three periods (1) Mauryan, (2) Śuṅga and (3) Sātavāhana-Kṣatrapa. The yield of beads was not much as only 25 beads have been recovered. The period wise distribution was as follows: Mauryan — 1 bead; Śuṅga — 4; Sātavāhana-Kṣatrapa — 16; and 4 unstratified beads.

These are made of agate, carnelian, chalcedony, crystal, garnet, glass, jasper and terracotta. In these, glass and terracotta beads predominate.

Quite a quantity of chipped nodules of agate, carnelian and garnet were found. In addition to these, a few unstratified beads were also available. These together indicate that beads were made locally at Paunī, at least in the early centuries of the Christian era.

The collared barrel bead of glass and the granulated white glass bead are in consonance in respect of their dating here as at other sites as well.

Prakāshe (21°30' N: 74°21'E) lies in Shāhādā *tāluka* of Dhūliā district and is situated on the confluence of the rivers Tāpī and Gomāi. It is enclosed within the sharp meander of the latter (Thapar 1967: 1-17; *IAR*, 54-5: 13).

Explorations at the site indicated that the Dark Age after the fall of the Indus civilisation and the beginning of early historic period could be filled up and so it was excavated.

B.K. Thapar of the Archaeological Survey of India did the vertical excavations during the months of February-April 1955.

The excavation exposed an occupational deposit of orderly stratification relating to four cultural periods beginning with (1) Chalcolithic and followed by (2) Mauryan, (3) Sātavāhana and (4)

Kṣatrapa period.

In the Chalcolithic period, along with other lapidary finds, were beads, variously of carnelian, shell and paste, including a distinct spacer and a chisel-ended toothpick or pendant. Beads, bangles and styli bespeak of a sedentary life with leisure for such arts and workmanship.

In the Mauryan levels, a cluster of twelve standard bicone hexagonal beads in rock crystal, five chevrons or chain beads in carnelian and a scabbard-type pendant in terracotta are particularly noteworthy for workmanship. Personal ornaments and domestic equipment's show development and sophistication.

Sātavāhana period did not introduce any revolutionary change in typology or material. Twenty-four beads were recovered from this period. Of these, the claw-shaped pendant in carnelian and mallet-shaped one in glass were outstanding.

In the Kṣatrapa levels, 51 beads were found. In this period glass industry showed an impulse towards large-scale production.

The materials used for bead-making in Prakashe include: agate, bone, carnelian, coral, glass, jasper, rock crystal, quartz, shell, paste and terracotta.

Sopārā (19° 25' N: 72° 45' E) lies on the western bank of Vasai creek, 37 miles north of Bombay, in Thāne district. It appears as a holy and wealthy city and an emporium in Aparanta (North Konkaṇa) from 250 BC to about CE 1500. It was a chief city as early as the times of Aśoka as here were engraved his rock edicts. Like several other places, Sopārā is honoured in Buddhist works as the birthplace of Gautama Buddha in one of his previous births (Cowell, *et. al.*: 1907). The *Mahābhārata* also mentions Surpāraka (Sopārā) (Bhagawanlal 1883: 304-5).

The Jaina writer Jinaprabhasūri, who flourished in the beginning of the fourteenth century, mentions Sopārā as one of the eighty-four holy places of the Jainas. Sopārā finds mention in various foreign writings, for example, Ptolemy (CE 150) mentions Sopārā between Nausaripur (Navasārī) and Simylla

(Chaul). At the beginning of the tenth century Al Masudi mentions Sopārā along with Thāne and Saimur as coastal towns. In 1049 Sopārā is mentioned as a port in a Śilāhāra grant.

Al Idrasi, in the middle of the twelfth century, describes Sopārā as a mile and half away from the sea with a great trade. He describes it as one of the emporia of India where pearl fishing was practised. Under the Portuguese, Sopārā was a fortified port with four wooden stockades (Ghate 1975).

Western Indian cave inscriptions contain six references to Sopārā. The author of the *Periplus of the Erythrean Sea* notices Sopārā as a local mart.

These references prove that Sopārā was one of the leading cities and trade-centres on the western coast of India.

Bhagawanlāl Indraji carried out vertical excavations on the Buruda Rājāchā Killa mound in April 1881. This mound gave remains of a Mauryan *stūpa*, which yielded a relic box of yellow tranchytic trap.

Thirty-one beads made of amethyst, beryl, crystal, gold and malachite were recovered. Distinct among the beads are *triratna* made of white-purple amethyst, undrilled hexagonal cylinders (to be held in metal caps) of deep blue glass and malachite and beryl fishes.

Ter (76°12'N: 18°19'E) in the district and *tāluka* of Osmānābād, is situated on both the banks of the river Terna.

Ter village, however, has long earned reputation as a site of archaeological interest owing to the richness of surface finds and a large number of important antiquities in local private collection. It has been identified with the ancient trade-centre Ṭagara (Chapekar 1969: i-vii, 1-7; Fleet 1901: 537-52; *IAR*, 57-8: 23-4).

The earliest literary reference is to be found in the *Periplus of the Erythraean Sea* written in the first century of the Christian era. Ptolemy, the Greek geographer writing about the middle of second century CE places Ṭagara in the region called Ariake.

Epigraphical evidences testify to the existence of this city from the seventh to seventeenth century CE. The city appears to have been under the rule of the Cālukyas, Śilāhāras and perhaps Muslim (*AR ASI*, 1901-2: 1; 1903-4: 21).

So Ter seems to have been consistently occupied since the dawn of the Christian era.

P.M. Joshi, Director of Archives and Historical Monuments, Government of Bombay, had in his view, the immense and promising archaeological potentialities of the site of Ter. Hence, at his instance, K.D. Banerjee and B.N. Chapekar carried out excavation in February 1958.

The excavation revealed that the site has been under occupation from *circa* third century BC to third century CE, i.e., in (1) Early Sātavāhana and (2) Indo-Roman periods. This excavation yielded one hundred and ninety-seven beads. Of these, 47 came from Period 1 and 144 from Period 2. These are made of agate, carnelian, chalcedony, crystal, faience, glass, jasper, lapis-lazuli, shell and terracotta. Routes connected Ter with other flourishing indigenous trading centres, viz., Bharoch, Koṇḍāpur, Nevāsā, Paiṭhan and Nāgārjunikoṇḍa. Trade contacts are also evident from the Kaolin figurines and lapis-lazuli beads since these materials are not locally available at Ter.

Of the varied shapes of beads, 'the faggot' shape appears to be new at Ter.

The Director of Archives and Museums resumed further excavation (*IAR*, 1967-8: 35; 1968-9: 17-18). This revealed the cultural sequence from pre-Mauryan to modern times. Both vertical and horizontal diggings were undertaken. This yielded a lion carved in shell, beads of various shapes in agate, carnelian, lapis-lazuli and shell.

S.B. Deo and T.V. Pathy of Deccan College and Marāṭhawāḍā University undertook the third and the most recent excavation, respectively. This was done to confirm the cultural sequence of the site, to assign the date of the Kaolin and terracotta figurines, and to know the nature of pre-Sātavāhana habitation, if any. This has given evidence of what was possibly a formidable wooden palisade around the city (*IAR*, 1974-5: 32).

Many other sites like Aundh, Chandā, Deoṭāk, Hiṅganghāṭ, Ite, Kalyān, Kānherī, Kapre, Katarpada, Junnar, Lohārī, Mahigāon, Nerle, Pimpalgāon, Sirpur, Tadoli, Tarhala, Vaḍgāon, have been partially excavated or explored known to yield Mauryan and Sātavāhana cultural remains (Map 2). However, reports of the excavations and exploration are not published adequately. Publication of such reports in future will bring to light many more specimens.

An overview of these excavated sites of Maharashtra tells us that bead-making was concentrated in the Sātavāhana period.

4

Probable Sources of Raw Materials

Now we shall study another important aspect, viz., sources of raw materials, as it helps in determining the status of the person using it. These throw flood light on the cultural contacts like migration of people, trade between the source place and the find spot of the stone amulets and pendants.

The Deccan Traps of western India are a great centre of agate, amethyst, carnelian, onyx, quartz and different varieties of chalcedony (Map 3).

In M. P. the geodes of the Deccan Traps contain varieties of agate, carnelian, opal, onyx, jasper. These are abundant in the bed of the Narmadā river (Wadia 1966).

The potential source of agate is from the mines of Rewā Kāṇṭhā, Rājpīpla, Ranpur and Kaira district of Gujarat, Bengal, Rājmahal and Singbhūm in Hyderabad, and Jabalpur in Madhya Pradesh. Agate is of common occurrence in the amygdoloidal basalts of the Deccan Traps, which covers extensive parts of Maharashtra.

Amethyst, occurs in outcrops of the Deccan Traps, in the bed of the Narmadā near Jabalpur, filling up lava-cavities, and in the Rājmahal traps of Burhait in the Santhāl Parganās, Bihar and Orissa (Brown: 1923). The mineral is also common in the Sutlej Valley in Bashar region, Punjab, and several localities in Andhra, Tamil Nadu (Wadia 1983), Chhindwārā and Wārangal districts, Central Provinces, Tanjore district, Madras, and Kumāun (Brown 1923). Dhārwār rock system is rich in amethyst (Wadia 1983).

In Gujarat State, the chief place, which supplies agate, is Ratanpur and Damlai in Rājpīpla where rolled pebbles of amygdaloids are contained in a tertiary conglomerate (Brown 1923).

Beryl, occurs in Mewar, Jodhpur and Ajmer in Rajasthan. Small quantities of beryl occur in the pegmatites of Rajasthan, Bihar and Andhra (Krishnan 1982).

The chief places for crystal, are Tanjore, Kālābāgh, and Kashmir (Wadia 1966).

Emerald, and aquamarine, occur in Mewar. Aquamarine is also available in Bihar, Nellore, Ajmer and Krishnagarh in Rajasthan (Wadia 1983).

Garnets, are most abundant in the metamorphosed rocks of Rajasthan. Its occurrence is confined mainly to Nellore, Krishnagarh, and Viśākhāpaṭnam districts of Andhra. In Madras, Garnet occurs in Ovari-Navaladi, Kuttankuli, Nīlgirī, Sālem district, Tiruchirapalli, Kanyākumarī, Rāmānāthapuram districts in Mysore. In Rajasthan it occurs in Sarwar, Rājmahal, Phulad districts. Garnets are of very common occurrence in Archeaon system (Wadia 1966). Many other localities are Gharibpeṭ, Wārangal, Khammamet districts in Hyderabad (Brown: 1923).

In Mysore State jasper, is found near Thimmapagarh in Sandur *tāluka* of Bellāry district.

Magnesite, is available in Sālem district of Madras and the Hasan and Mysore districts in Karnataka. The best known occurrences are those of chalk hills near Sālem and of Koḍakole in Mysore (Krishnan 1982).

Pegmatites, carrying flespar, quartz, and mica, are seen at a number of places in Maharashtra like Ratnagiri, Chandā, Nāgpur, Bhanḍārā.

Workable deposits of steatite, occur in Singhbhūm district of Bihar, Jabbalpur, Sālem, Idār, Jaipur, Archaeon and Dhārwār rocks of the Peninsula (Wadia 1983).

True jade, comes into India from the Karakash Valley of south Turkistan and China (Wadia 1983).

Yellow tranchytic trap, found in the Nīlā hill, about a mile east of Sopārā and also near Kurlā in Salsette (Bhagwanlal 1881).

It is quite possible that the authors of Mauryan and Sātavāhana cultures in Maharashtra might have obtained their raw material from the above named sources, either themselves or through intermediaries (Map 2).

5

Amulets and Pendants

A Typological Study

JEWELLRY is worn to adorn human body and tastefulness forms the key-note in jewellery designs; but very often designs in jewellery forms do not convey any pleasing note or display any artistic quality. These designs have a place of their own. They are traced in ornaments, almost all over the world from a very early age. Most of these designs are associated with some common belief, magic or religious ideas and many have a deep significance.

Human belief in magical symbols contained in geometric or other designs is very old. In course of time, these designs came to be incorporated in portable charms — so that the potent in them could be easily carried on persons, and thus amulets and pendants came into being.

An 'amulet' is defined as an object supposed by superstitions to protect its possessor from evil, mischief, bad luck, sickness, accident, disaster, or witchcraft (*Encyclopedia Americana*, Vol. 1, 594).

A 'pendant' is defined as a hanging jewel, etc., especially one attached to a necklace, bracelet, etc. (*The Concise Oxford Dictionary*, 880).

It is natural to ask why amulets and pendants are so numerous and so widely distributed. With the passage of time, man's fear of evil spirits did not diminish, on the contrary it increased, and each generation became more and more devil-ridden than its predecessor.

In Maharashtra, amulets are found to have been worn from as early as the Chalcolithic age. During the early Historic Period, quite a variety of pendants were in vogue. A large number of them have been reported from sites in Maharashtra datable to *circa* third century BC to the third century CE.

It is difficult to afford explanation for each and every amuletic form found in excavation, but pursuit of the forms in them is interesting.

In order to be clear and to distinguish the importance of pendants and amulets, they are dealt with separately here.

Pendants

Pendants are of simple and conventional shapes without any particular importance, i.e., they are basically for decorative purposes. They exhibit a variety of shapes. In the following pages they are classified and arranged in alphabetical order.

BUD PENDANTS

Four specimens of bud pendants are reported in Maharashtra. All the four have come form Kauṇḍinyapura and belong to the Sātavāhana period. Three specimens are made of shell (*fig*. 2.2), (Dikshit 1968: Pl. XXXIV-7,8,9) and one is made of steatite (*fig*. 2.1) (Dikshit 1968: fig. 32-15). 'L'-shaped perforation characterises these specimens. These pointed bud pendants may have been used as terminals at the lower end of the necklaces. This is the reason why they bear 'right-angled' perforation.

CLUB PENDANTS

The only specimen so far of club pendant comes from Bhokardan (Deo and Gupte 1974: fig. 23-100; 131-2). It is made from bubbly glass. It is attributed to the third century CE. It is cylindrical with tapering sides. The broader end is perforated and the narrow one has a broad base (*fig*. 2.3).

CONICAL PENDANT

Two conical pendants have so far been reported one each from Nāsik and Nevāsā.

Nevāsā specimen (Sankalia, *et.al.* 1960: fig. 194.6) is a piece of horn, triangular in outline, with a perforation at the apex. Another partial perforation is at the base. It is datable to second century BC (*fig*. 2.4).

Nāsik specimen belongs to the medieval period. This is in Terracotta. It is a conical, flat based specimen with smooth base. The base has a pair of incised lines forming a plus sign. The top is truncated and has a hole (*fig*. 2.5).

CRESCENT-SHAPED PENDANT

Brahmapurī has yielded a crescent-shaped pendant belonging to the Sātavāhana period (Sankalia and Dikshit 1952: Pl. XXVI. B.2 96-7). It is made of terracotta, cast from a mould and decorated with two bands of beadings arranged in the shape of a cross superimposed by a small deeply incised pellet in the central portion of the specimen. It is attributed to the Sātavāhana period.

Bhokardan has yielded a few with decoration, such as semi-circular lines, floral designs stepped up pellets and dots, beaded lines, etc. (Deo and Gupte 1974: fig. 29.1-12, 154-5).

DOUBLE-CAPPED PENDANT

A double-capped crystal pendant is reported from Nāsik (Sankalia and Deo 1955: fig. 45.7). It bears slightly hexagonal sides, with a number of slanting lines incised on both surfaces to give the effect of decoration. It is perforated at the base of the upper cap and bears polished surface (*fig*. 2.6).

DROP PENDANTS

Drop pendants are of wide occurrence and have been reported from Ahicchatra, Arikāmeḍu, Bhir-Mouṇḍ, Kośam, Maheśvar, Māskī, Taxilā, Vaiśālī and Nāsik, Nevāsā and Paunār in Maharashtra.

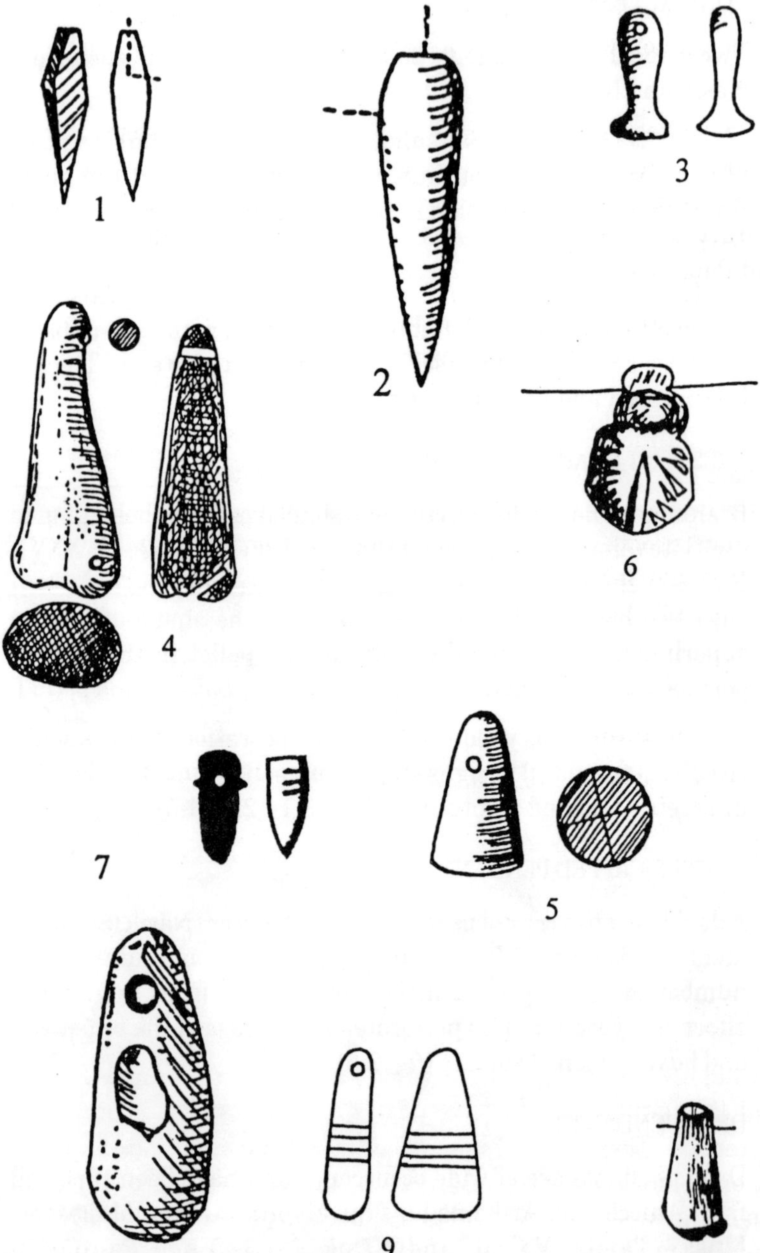

FIGURE - 2.

They possess a bulbous (of the shape of the drop of water) lower portion with a perforated top. Some even have tapering ends.

Seventeen specimens have been reported from Brahmapurī, Bhokardan, Nāsik, Nevāsā and Paunār excavations in Maharashtra. The earliest specimen is assignable to the second century BC from Nevāsā. Two specimens each from Bhokardan and Paunār are from surface scatters.

A variety of materials has been used like agate, amethyst, blue faience, carnelian, chalcedony, crystal, glass, ivory, jasper, opal and terracotta.

A specimen from Nevāsā (Sankalia, *et. al.* 1960: fig. 167-11) of pale blue faience is an inverted drop pendant (*fig.* 2.7). It is dated between first century BC and third century CE. It bears two shallow grooves at the broader end. The other end is very pointed. Similar specimens are reported from Sirkap in carnelian and quartz (Beck: 1941).

Another specimen from Nevāsā (Sankalia, *et. al.* 1960: fig. 168.25) is of red jasper. It is assigned to the second century BC. It is a very beautiful specimen with a more rounded form (*fig.* 2.8).

Four specimens have been recovered from Bhokardan. Out of these, two in (Deo and Gupte 1974: fig. 20.12-13) banded agate are from surface (*fig.* 2.9). The material is very carefully selected. The third specimen is of carnelian (Deo and Gupte 1974: fig. 21-4) and assigned to the third century CE. It is similar to the Nevāsā red jasper specimen.

Specimen in opal from Nāsik (Sankalia and Deo 1955: fig. 45.15) is assigned between 200 BC and 400 CE bracket (*fig.* 2.10). Two identical drop pendants have been found at Paunār (Deo and Dhavalikar 1968: fig. 28.4) (*fig.* 3.1). These are made of terracotta. They are complete pendants with cylindrical shape, tapering sides, flat circular faces and with perforation near the top of the tapering end. The third specimen from Paunār (Deo and Dhavalikar 1968: fig. 24.12) (*fig.* 3.2), in carnelian is a fragmentary one.

The fourth specimen in chalcedony is a complete one. It is a tapering cylinder with convex ends. It bears perforation near the narrow end. It has come from surface scatters (Deo and Dhavalikar 1968: fig. 24.17) (*fig*. 3.3). Bhokardan has yielded a similar one in glass. It is attributed to *c*. CE 100-200. Carnelian specimen from Paunār is attributed to the third century CE.

A specimen from Kauṇḍinyapura (Dikshit 1968: fig. 32.25) is of crystal with a 'L' perforation.

A single one in ivory at Nevāsā (Sankalia, *et. al.* 1960: fig. 198.1) with flat base and truncated top is the only one known in ivory.

Two drop pendants have been recovered from Brahmapurī in carnelian (Sankalia and Dikshit 1952: fig. 30.11). These are identical specimens with bulbous body and flat top where it is perforated. The carnelian one belongs to the Sātavāhana period, whereas the amethyst one is attributed to the Bahmanī period. This shows that they were popular for quite a longer span of time.

Thus, the drop pendants in Maharashtra seem to have survived till the medieval period, but they seem to have been more popular in the Sātavāhana period.

MALLET-SHAPED PENDANT

The only specimen of a mallet-shaped pendant has been reported from Prakāshe. It is assignable to 600-200 BC levels. Made from green copper-coloured glass, it is translucent (Thapar 1967: fig. 38.34). It is cylindrical but tapering at one end. The tapering end culminates in a small circle at the top in which there is a perforation (*fig* 3.4).

RECTANGULAR TABULAR PENDANT

Three specimens of rectangular tabular pendants have come from Brahmapurī. These belong to the Sātavāhana period. These are made from well levigated clay.

The first specimen (Sankalia and Dikshit 1952: Pl. XXVI-A3) is rectangular in shape and decorated with a number of beadings in high relief enclosed within borders. This pattern is executed in a mould and the design is the same on both the sides (*fig*. 3.5).

The other two (Sankalia and Dikshit 1952: Pl. XIX) are fragmentary and trapezoid in shape. They are decorated with heart-shaped motifs and beadings. This design is in high relief. On the reverse, fingerprints of the maker indicate that they were cast from a mould (*fig*. 3.6).

SCABBARD PENDANT

A terracotta scabbard pendant (Thapar 1967: fig. 38.41) (*fig*. 3.7), is reported from Prakashe from a late level of the Mauryan period. It is a delicately moulded specimen with a neat perforation through the hilt.

SHELL PENDANT

In Maharashtra, two specimens of shell used as pendants have been reported from Kauṇḍinyapura (*fig*. 3.8).

In these (Dikshit 1968: Pl. XXXIV-3), the bivalve of a shell was used as a pendant by drilling a small hole at its apex. These are attributed to the Mauryan periods.

SPACER PENDANT

One spacer pendant is reported from Brahmapurī (Sankalia and Dikshit 1952: Pl. XXVI-A.2), (*fig*. 3.9). Recovered from Sātavāhana stratum, it is a specimen in pottery with a deep brown slip. It bears an ornamental device in the shape of horizontal and vertical flutes or ribbings at the top, and an elongated tapering body below. The lower portion of this pendant is broken and the underside is flat. Two holes in the upper portion show that it was a spacer bead-pendant.

This type of bead-*cum*-pendant seems to have been popular in the Sātavāhana period. Several pendants of the same

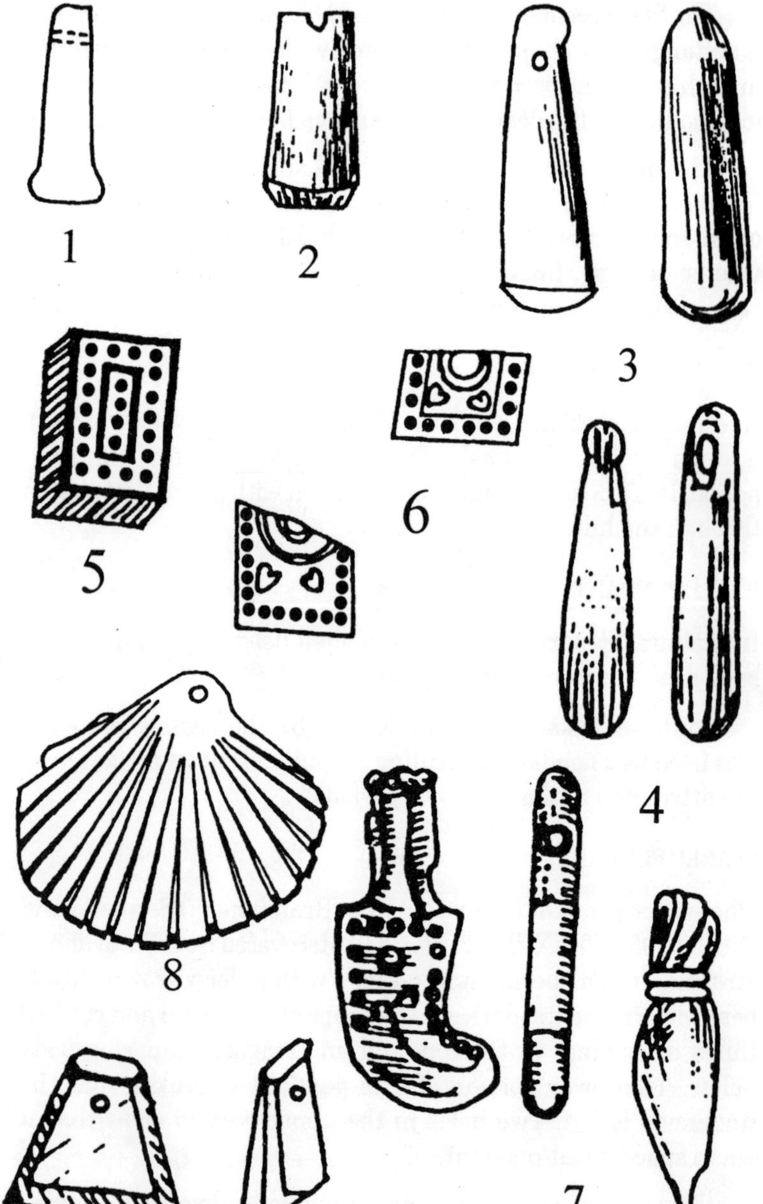

FIGURE - 3.

description are known from Koṇḍāpur in Andhra Pradesh. Sometimes the lower register is decorated with a fluted *amalaka* or clustered beadings. One such from Karaḍ is deposited in the Bhāratīya Itihāsa Saṁśodhan Maṇḍal, Pune.

TRIANGULAR PENDANT

Two triangular pendants are reported from Nāsik. They are dated between 400 and 200 BC.

Nāsik has given a fine, smooth, tabular pendant of deep red carnelian (Sankalia and Deo 1955: fig. 45.19). It is perforated near the truncated top. It is slightly worn out on one face (*fig*. 3.10).

Another specimen is made of shell (Sankalia and Deo 1955: fig. 46.5). It is also a tabular triangular pendant. It is thicker at the top where it is perforated. It is smooth and polished (*fig*. 4.1).

A third specimen has been recovered from Nevāsā. This coral specimen is in its natural state (Sankalia, *et. al*. 1960: fig. 166-151). It is ascribed to the second century BC (*fig*. 4.2).

MISCELLANEOUS PENDANTS

Five specimens are unclassified. These are recovered from Nevāsā, Bhokardan, Paunār and Ter. These are made from carnelian, chalcedony, ivory and terracotta.

The chalcedony specimen from Nevāsā is a neatly perforated natural nodule recovered from chalcolithic levels (*fig*. 4.3). Perforation from both the sides has resulted in a hole of hourglass section (Sankalia, *et. al*. 1960: fig. 166.14).

The second specimen from Nevāsā is made from ivory (Sankalia, *et. al*. 1960: fig. 198.11). It is datable between *c*. first century BC and second and third century CE. It is a flat-based piece of ivory with the top truncated. It bears a neat perforation near the head (*fig*. 4.4).

An unclassified terracotta specimen from Paunar is dated to

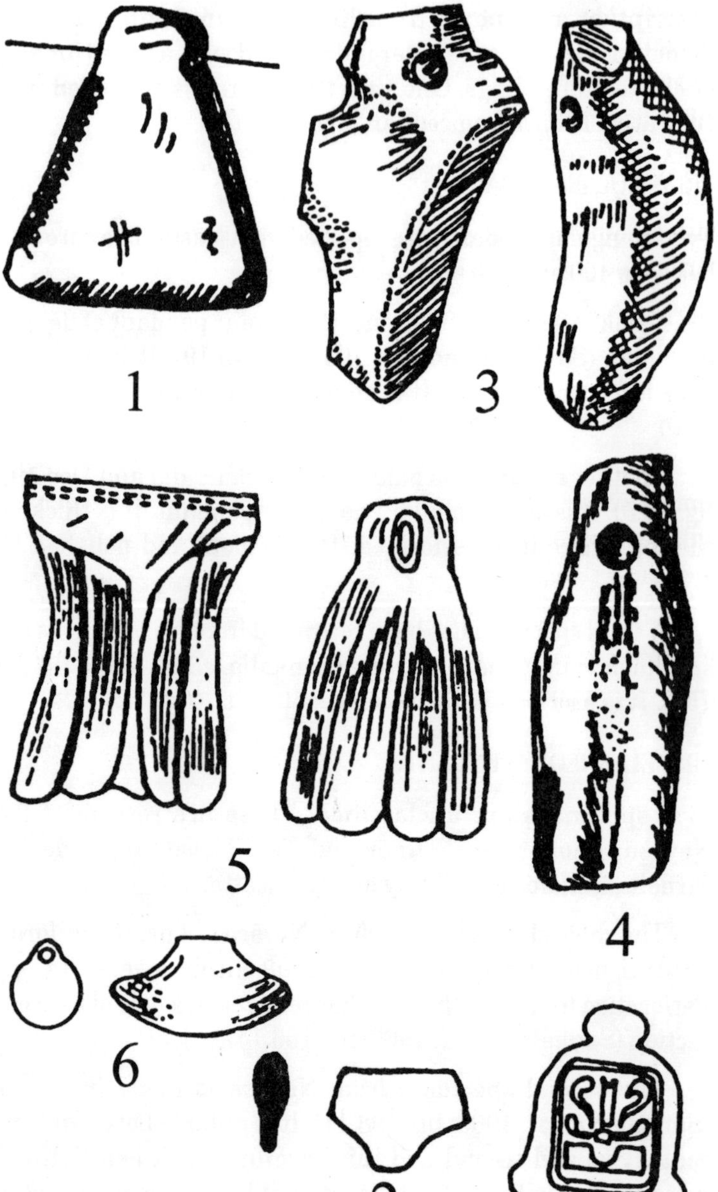

FIGURE - 4.

the third century CE (Deo and Dhavalikar 1968: fig. 25.47). This pendant has a vertically ribbed cylindrical body, with sideways projections, which are horizontally perforated, and with the base concave (*fig*. 4.5).

Another unclassified specimen from Bhokardan is a surface find (Deo and Gupte 1974: fig. 21.39). This lenticular pendant with a hump is made of carnelian. This bears high polish and is perforated through the hump (*fig*. 4.6).

The fifth specimen is from Ter and made of terracotta (*fig*. 4.7). It is a bell-shaped pendant with some decoration within a border.

Amulets

Amulets are worn to ward off bad luck or such influences as the evil eye, mischief, disease, witchcraft, etc. It is a means of defense and protection.

During the Mauryan and the Sātavāhana periods, a variety of amulets have been found from the excavations in Maharashtra. These are made of various materials.

These amulets reflect the religious and social beliefs of contemporary times. These can be grouped into the following:

<table>
<tr><td colspan="6">Amulets with animals and their components representation</td></tr>
<tr><td colspan="2">Bull amulets</td><td colspan="2">Fish amulets</td><td colspan="2">Lion amulets</td></tr>
<tr><td colspan="2">Makara amulets</td><td colspan="2">Claw amulets</td><td colspan="2">Tortoise amulets</td></tr>
<tr><td colspan="6">Amulets with artifactual representation</td></tr>
<tr><td colspan="6">Dagger amulets</td></tr>
<tr><td colspan="6">Amulets with human body and its components as amulets</td></tr>
<tr><td colspan="3">Eye beads</td><td colspan="3">Tooth amulets</td></tr>
<tr><td colspan="3">Human-figure amulets</td><td colspan="3">Yaksa amulets</td></tr>
</table>

Amulets with religious symbols		
1Heart-shaped amulets	Conch-shell amulets	
Pīpal-leaf amulets,	Triratna amulets	
Casket amulets	Stūpa amulets,	Nandīpada amulets
Miscellaneous		
Cylindrical amulets (Tāveez)		

Amulets with animals and their components representation

BULL AMULETS

Bull amulets are known from a number of sites in India. These are made of a variety of materials, but popularity and larger shape in terracotta are evidenced by the specimens encountered in Maharashtra. Nine specimens have been reported from sites in this region. They are from Bhokardan, Nevāsā, Paiṭhan and Ter.

Ter specimens (Chapekar 1969: fig. 30.52-4; Deo Ter: fig. 50) (*fig*. 5.1), are dated to the Sātavāhana period. All these show humped bull in a sitting posture. The bull is facing right and has a cord around the neck and the hump. A kind of decorated pedestal is provided for each of them. One of them has a lotus pedestal. The perforation runs horizontally through the pedestal. Due to the weight of the body and the basal perforation, the animal would always be placed upside down when the amulet was hung round the neck of the wearer. These are made in double moulds.

Nevāsā specimen (Sankalia, *et. al*. 1960: fig. 170-8) has larger dimensions but it is quite similar to the Ter specimens. It is dated to the first century CE (*fig*. 5.2).

Paiṭhan amulet is dated to the Sātavāhana period (Dhavalikar 1966: Pl. XXV.16). Here a bull made of kaolin and executed from a double mould is shown sitting on a platform. It has two large chains around the neck; of these, one is around the neck and the other passes behind the hump. The bull is of the short horn variety and the dewlap is indicated realistically (*fig*. 5.3). Its size

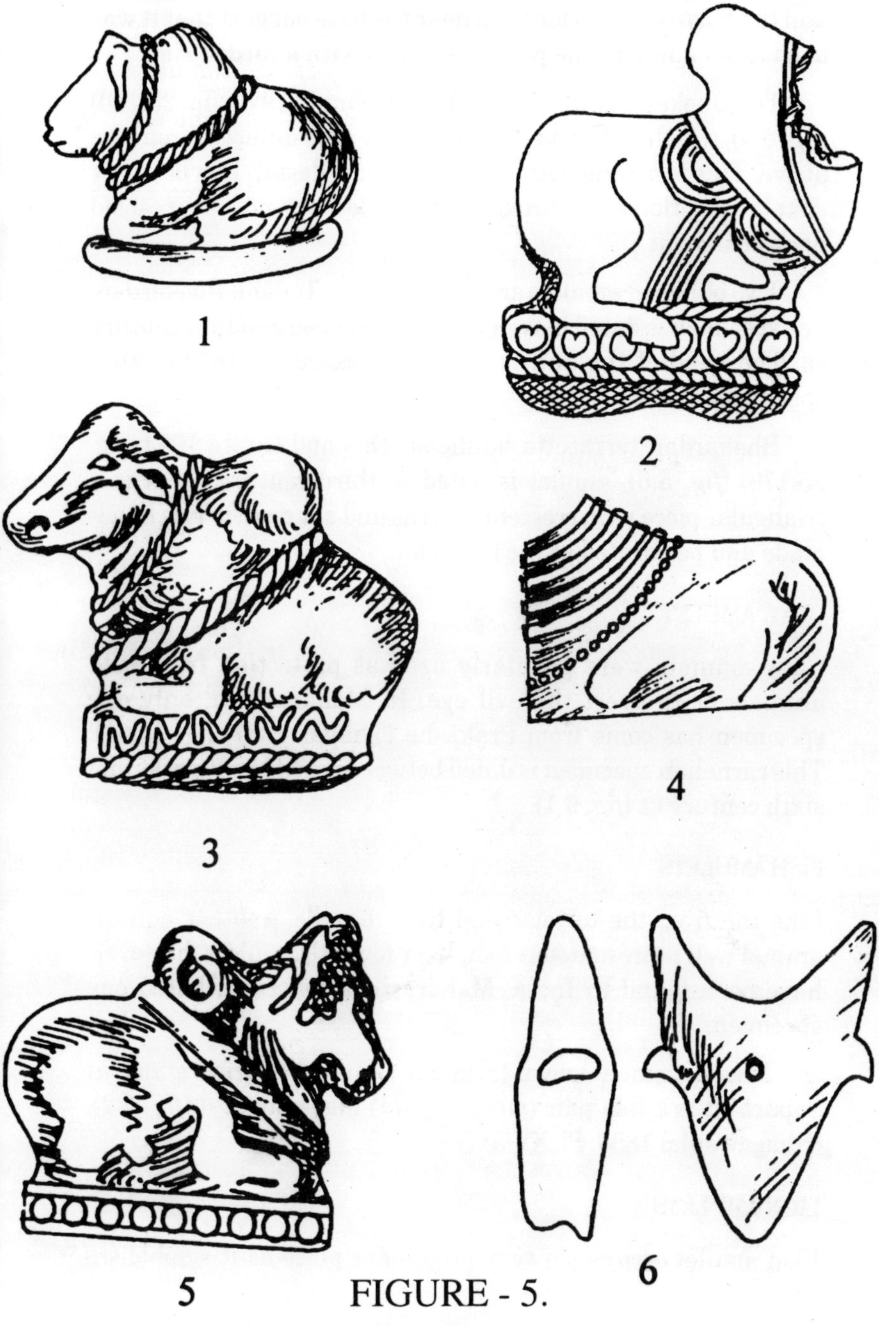

FIGURE - 5.

and the horizontal perforation near the base suggest that it was used as an amulet. The pedestal is oval with a corded rim.

The Bhokardan specimen (Deo and Gupte 1974: fig. 25.180) (*fig*. 5.4), which is dated to third century CE is different from the above. This is a humpless bull without a pedestal. It is of a very simple execution and is broken. It has a dewlap and a long cabled neck ornament.

Two bullhead amulets are reported from Ter and Bhokardan. Ter specimen is dated between first century BC and first century CE. The head of the bull is similar in execution to the other specimens (*fig*. 5.5).

Bhokardan terracotta bullhead (Deo and Gupte 1974: fig. 25.179) (*fig*. 5.6), amulet is dated to third century CE. It is a triangular piece with crescentic horns and slit mouth. It is hand-made and perforated at the forehead.

CLAW AMULET

Claw amulets were popularly used as protection from wild animals or to avert the evil eye. In Maharashtra, only one specimen has come from Prakāshe (Thapar 1967: fig. 38.36). This carnelian specimen is dated between second century BC and sixth century CE (*fig*. 6.1).

FISH AMULETS

Like the frog, the tortoise and the crocodile, another aquatic animal well represented is fish. Very few fish amulets, however, have been found in India. Maharashtra has contributed one specimen.

This specimen comes from the Mauryan period *stūpa* at Sopārā. It is a fish pair (*mīna-yugala*) made of beryl (*fig*. 6.2), (Bhagawanlal 1883: Pl. XV.3).

LION AMULETS

Lion amulet occupies a very prominent place as it symbolises power. Besides this, on the sites with Buddhist associations, it can be interpreted to represent the Buddha, who is reckoned as the lion of the Śākya race (*śākyasiṁha*). All the amulets represent the full figure of the animal. Stratified specimens are found at Nāsik and Ter.

The specimen from Nāsik is made of polished crystal, (Sankalia and Deo 1955: Pl. XXI-2) depicting a couchant lion with (*fig*. 6.3) perforation near the chest. Delicately made, it is dated between 200 BC and CE 400. Its tail is curved and broken. The other end shows the foreleg, the mouth, the eyes and the mane. This site has also yielded one specimen in garnet.

Ter (*IAR*, 1967-68: 35) has yielded one such in shell. It is assignable to the late Sātavāhana period, *c*. CE 100-200.

MAKARA AMULETS

Among the major groups of animals represented in Indian art, the *makaras* are found rarely as amulets.

Only a few specimens of *makara* amulets have come down to us. In Maharashtra, two specimens are reported, one each from Bhokardan and Nevāsā (*fig*. 6.4). These are assigned to the third century CE.

Both the specimens, made of terracotta, are fashioned in a mould. *Makara-mukha* is at either terminal with open mouth. Perforation is along the shorter axis and through one *mukha* only.

TORTOISE AMULETS

Tortoise-shaped amulets are very common all over India. It has a time worn antiquity. Dikshit (Dikshit 1968: 97) states that during the early centuries of the Christian era it was in vogue. The earliest specimen is reported from Maharashtra. It is assigned to *c*.1700 BC (Chalcolithic period), at Prakāshe (Thapar 1967: fig. 37.31).

Five specimens have been reported from excavated sites in

Maharashtra. These specimens are from Prakāshe, Ter, Bhokardan and Kauṇḍinyapura. The materials used are shell and faience.

Two specimens in faience from Ter (Chapekar 1969: fig. 30.7) (*fig*. 6.5) and Kauṇḍinyapura (Dikshit 1968: Pl. XLVIII.G) (*fig*. 6.6), are attributed to the Sātavāhana period. The Kauṇḍinyapura specimen is a very fine piece and speaks of its quality. It has a perforation across the body in between the pair of legs.

Shell specimens belonging to the Sātavāhana period are flat and very simple, exhibiting inferior workmanship. They are prepared from a thick concave shell piece and show triangular head and short legs, as for example, the Bhokardan specimens (Deo and Gupte 1974: fig. 24.144, 145) (*fig*. 6.7-8). In course of time, it appears to get conventionalised; hence in later period we get flat specimens without much workmanship.

Several specimens have been reported from Nevāsā attributable between *c*. 150 BC and CE 200 (Dikshit 1968: 97). The Prakāshe specimen is made from the core of the shell as it is very thick. The head of the specimen is very long and pointed as compared to other specimens (*fig*. 6.8). As stated above, it is attributed to 1700 CE.

Amulets with artifactual representation

DAGGER AMULETS

Dagger amulets have wide distribution in Maharashtra. Four specimens have been reported from excavated sites. Two of these have come from Nevāsā. Both are assignable to second century BC. One specimen is made of blue glazed faience (Sankalia, *et. al.* 1960: fig. 195.14c) (*fig*. 6.9). It is a small dagger-like amulet with an indeterminate shape with a tapering point. Its one end is pointed and the other bulbous and perforated.

The second specimen is made of copper (Sankalia, *et. al.* 1960: fig. 167.1) (*fig*. 6.10). It is heavily rusted, the tip is broken and it has a flat broad hilt. At Nāsik, a dagger-shaped amulet of glass, having a lion head at the top, was found associated with

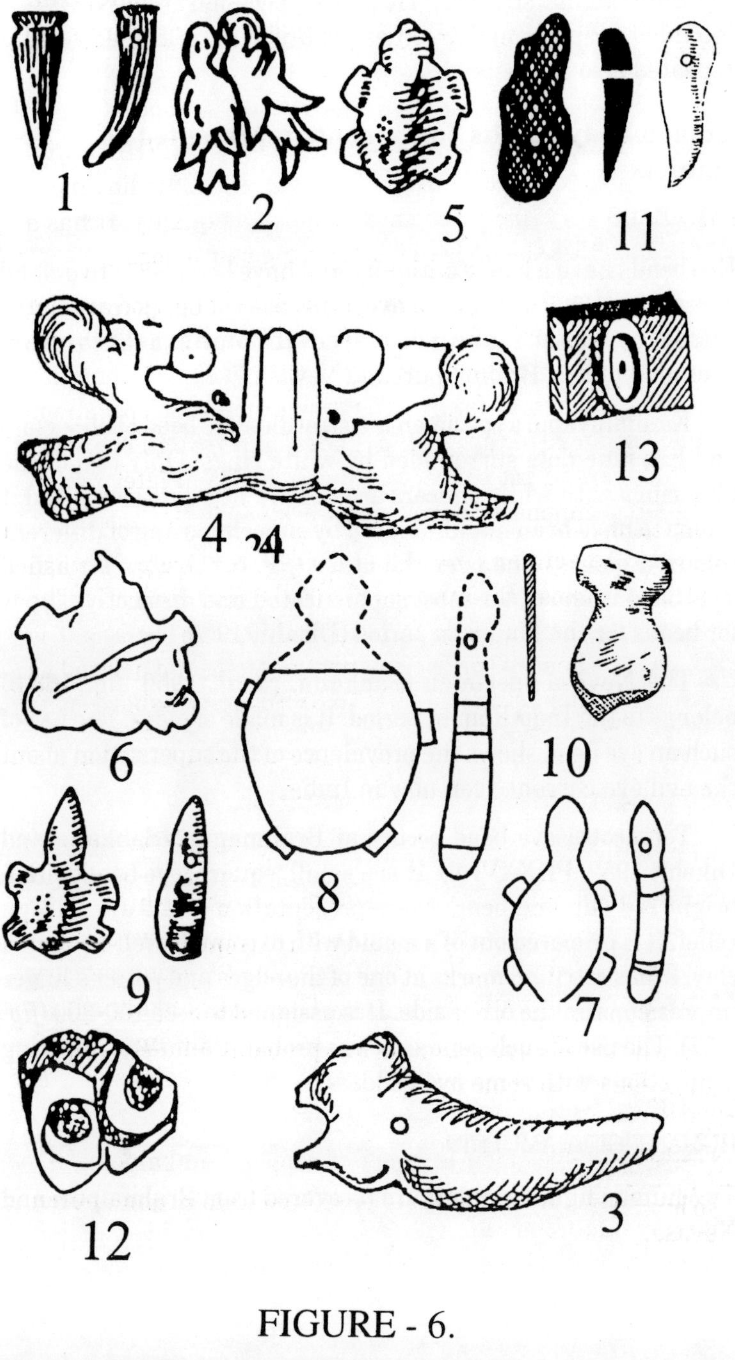

FIGURE - 6.

the Sātavāhana stratum. The shell specimen from Nevāsā is intended as spacer and assumes a characteristic shape, which is repeated also at Nāsik.

Human body and its components represented as amulets

EYE BEADS

Eye beads have a hoary antiquity and have been worn to defend oneself from evil eye and to avert diseases of dangerous kinds. Three eye-beads are recovered in Maharashtra from Kauṇḍinyapura, Brahmapurī and Nevāsā.

Kauṇḍinyapura specimen is a stratified eye bead of blue glass and has blue dots surrounded by white rings. Only two of the blue rings with white saucers around are now preserved and it seems to have been manufactured by superimposing of different coloured glasses one over the other (*fig.* 6.11). This stratified 'eye' bead is one of the most sophisticated and distinctive types for beads for the Mauryan period (Dikshit 1968: 99).

The Nevāsā specimen (Sankalia, *et. al.* 1960: fig. 168.3) belongs to the Indo-Roman period. It is made of glass. The use of such an eye bead shows the prevalence of the superstition about the evil eye current even now in India.

Terracotta eye bead occurs at Brahmapurī (Sankalia and Dikshit 1952: Pl. XXVI-6). It is a small, square, eye bead with a bright red slip and bears the representation of the eye in high relief. It is prepared out of a mould with extremely well-levigated clay. It has attrition marks at one of the edges and potter's finger impressions on the other side. It is assigned to *c.* CE 100-300 (*fig.* 6.12). The use of such pendants was probably amuletic implying connections with some eye goddess.

HUMAN FIGURE AMULETS

Two human figure amulets are recovered from Brahmapurı and Nevāsā.

Brahmapurī specimen shows a human figure in a seated posture with its head upraised. This lapis-lazuli specimen is attributed to the Sātavāhana period. It is prepared out of a fine-mottled stone and the limbs are fashioned by sawing with a sharp instrument, particularly to be noticed in the fashioning of the nose. It is about 1 and ½ inch in height (Sankalia and Dikshit 1952: 92). Nevāsā specimen is the outline of a human figure with several incised circles on the surface (Sankalia, *et. al*. 1960: fig. 169.11). It is dated between first century BC and third century CE. It is made of shell. Several incised circles were possibly made for inlay and the entire idea of this specimen must have been amuletic implying connection with some eye-goddess or for warding of small pox (*fig*. 7.1).

TOOTH AMULETS

Tooth amulets have long been known to possess talismanic value and were probably used for witchcraft purposes or for tooth cure. Six specimens have come to light from the excavations at Bhokardan, Prakashe and Nevāsā.

These are made of faience, chalcedony, shell and terracotta. Four specimens recovered from Bhokardan are made of chalcedony, faience, shell and terracotta. These are from the strata dated between first century BC and third century CE.

Bhokardan terracotta specimen is tapering downwards, the upper end is flat and bears a perforation (Deo and Gupte 1974: fig. 25.174) (*fig*. 7.2). The second specimen is made of blue faience. This is also tapering. It has a truncated flat top with two incised grooves (Deo and Gupte 1974: fig. 22.74) (*fig*. 7.3). The third specimen of chalcedony is thin, well executed tapering and perforated at the broader end (Deo and Gupte 1974: fig. 22.5) (*fig*. 7.4). The fourth specimen in shell is a very simple one (Deo and Gupte 1974: fig. 24.147) (*fig*. 7.5).

The last specimen from Nevāsā is of shell. It is slightly curved and tapering. On one surface there are three incised dots possibly for inlay. It has a breathwise 'L' perforation. Its top is flat and truncated (Sankalia, *et. al.* 1960: 373) (*fig.* 7.6).

YAKṢA AMULETS

Nevāsā has yielded one *yakṣa* amulet in terracotta, which is assigned between the first century BC and second and third century CE (Sankalia, *et. al.* 1960: fig. 170.8). It is a standing human figure with the head broken and perforated through the shoulders and the neck. This figure is wearing a *dhotī* with ends hanging, and a loose bunian like garment covering the body. The hands are folded and hold a round object over the belly. Navel is shown by a depression. There are amulets on arms and pendant on the chest. The reverse shows its back covered with a loose bunian (*fig.* 7.7).

CASKET-SHAPED AMULET

One casket-shaped amulet is recovered from Paunar, this calcite specimen is attributed to the third century CE (Deo & Dhavalikar 1968: Pl. XXVII.4) (*fig.* 7.8).

CONCH-SHELL AMULET

Single specimen of conch-shell is reported from Nāsik. It is dated from 200 to 400 BC. It is bored at the top (Sankalia and Deo 1955: No. 5188) (*fig.* 7.9).

HEART-SHAPED AMULET

A very interesting amulet is recovered from Paunār (Deo & Dhavalikar 1968: fig. 24.18). It is a heart-shaped chalcedony amulet with the figure of a seated Buddha on one face and incised decoration on the other. It is vertically perforated. Heart shape may be considered as a *pīpal* leaf, which will give this particular amulet immense importance (*fig.* 8.1).

NANDĪPADA AMULETS

The *nandīpada* (taurine) symbol is associated with Śaivism. The followers of Buddha as a symbol of their trinity adopted it.

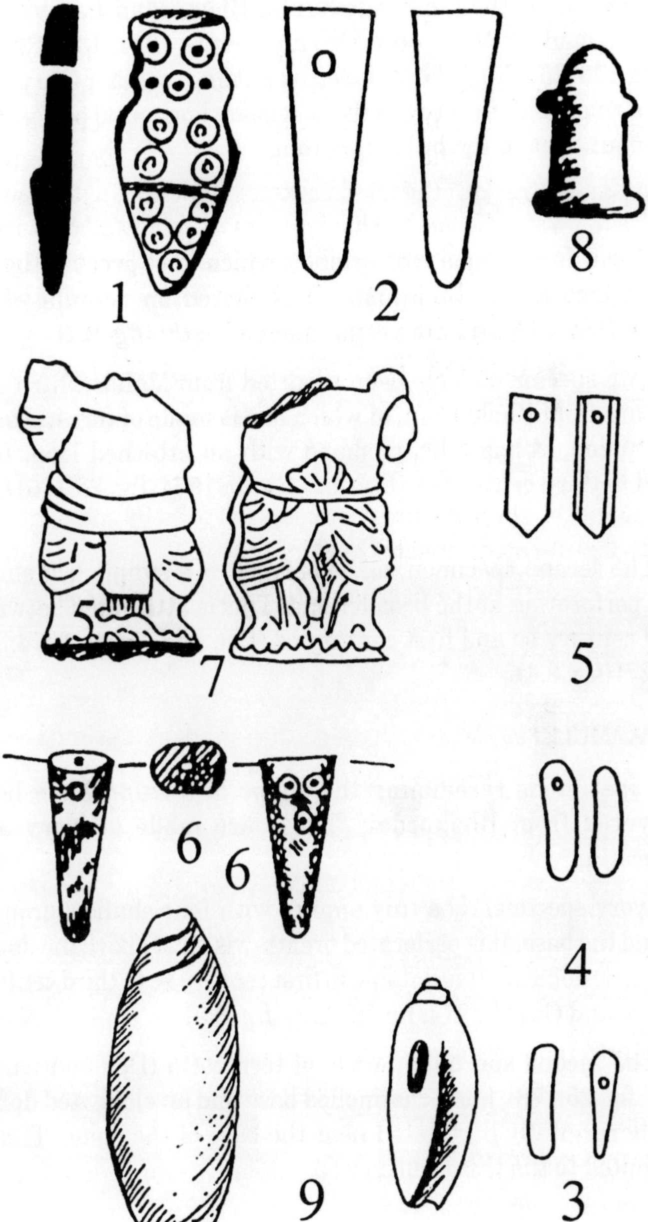

FIGURE - 7.

Nandīpada and *triratna* are indistinguishable in the shape and similar in their main features. Bhokardan had yielded amulets made in terracotta (Deo and Gupte 1974: 135, 139-40; fig. 23.128; 25.178). It is produced by putting together two pieces with a small stick in between them. It bears horizontal perforation at the junction of the bulb and prongs.

PĪPAL LEAF AMULETS

Pīpal leaf is an important symbol, which is of great religious importance to the Buddhists. It is sacred on account of its association with Buddha's attainment of *bodhi* (*fig*. 8.2).

Two specimens have been reported from Maharashtra and both are from Bhokardan, of which one is made of terracotta. It is moulded. It has a heart shape with an attached loop. It is dated to third century CE (Deo and Gupte 1974: fig. 25.175) (*fig*. 8.3).

The second specimen, made of ivory, is a simple leaf shape with perforation at the broader end. This is attributed between third century BC and first century CE (Deo and Gupte 1974: fig. 23.127) (*fig*. 8.4).

STŪPA AMULET

Two specimens resembling the shape of a *stūpa* have been recovered from Bhokardan. These are made of ivory and terracotta.

Ivory specimen is a tiny amulet with four shallow grooves around the base. It is perforated breath-wise just above the dome. The top is domical. It is datable to first century BC to third century CE (Deo and Gupte 1974: fig. 23.128) (*fig*. 8.5).

The second specimen, made of terracotta (Deo and Gupte 1974: fig. 25.178), has a channelled base and an elongated dome. It is horizontally perforated near the base of the dome. This is attributed to the third century CE.

TRIRATNA AMULETS

Triratna is one of the earliest motifs adopted by the followers of the Buddha for veneration and worship. It represents the triad of Buddhism: Buddha, *Dharma* and *Saṁgha*. It is shaped like a globular bead with three pronged attachments, the central one being short. Many of the sites, where this amulet has been reported, were also important centres of Buddhism, where many Buddhist monuments were erected and which became place of pilgrimage.

Two of them made in amethyst and beryl is known from Sopārā *stūpa* (Bhagawanlal 1883: 273, Pl. XV.4) (*fig.* 8.6). This is attributed to the Mauryan period. Those made of terracotta occur at Bhokardan. These are ascribed to *c.* 100 BC-CE 200 bracket (Deo and Gupte 1974: *fig.* 25.176,177) (*fig.* 8.7). But these are classified as *nandīpada*.

A terracotta specimen is known from Paunār (Deo and Dhavalikar 1960: 85, fig. 25.48). It is from surface scatters (*fig.* 8.8).

One specimen in glass is discovered from Ter (B.I.S. 1972: Vol.9 No.33-34: 29). This is also attributed to Sātavāhana period. This amulet is made by rubbing the glass. It is a noteworthy specimen.

Another specimen is known from Arṇī (*IAR*, 1984-85: 55). It is attributed to the Sātavāhana period.

*Triratna*s are also known from Nāsik, Nevāsā, Prakāshe and Paithan.

Miscellaneous

CYLINDRICAL AMULETS (TĀVEEZ)

Seven specimens are known from Bhokardan, Brahmapurī Kauṇḍinyapura, Sopārā and Ter. These are all attributed to the Sātavāhana period.

Except blue glass Sopārā specimen the material used is

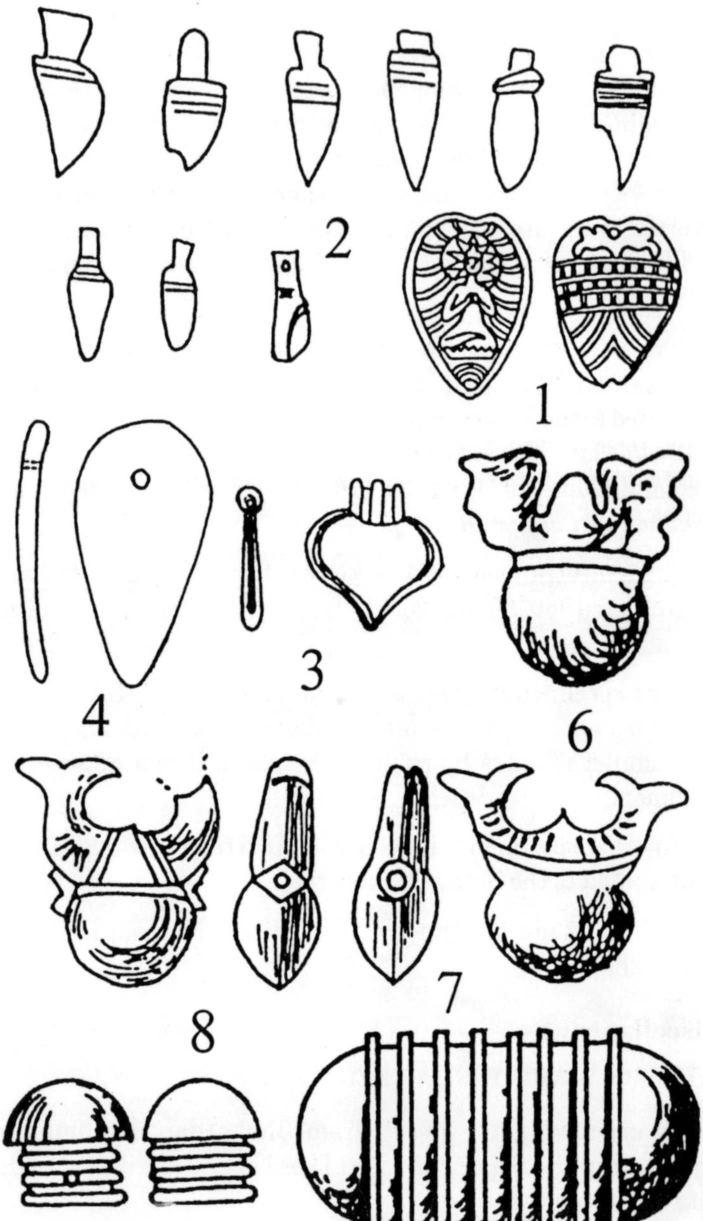

FIGURE - 8.

terracotta, which may point towards its wide prevalence. As the poor could not afford these amulets in metal or stone, they possibly copied it in a cheaper material like terracotta.

Two specimens attributed to the Sātavāhana period, one each from Ter and Brahmapurī, are typical amulets with a number of ribbings on the cylindrical body. These unperforated cylinders have convex ends. Therefore these must have been equipped with capped ends with two rings attached on both the sides for suspensions, as is evident from the specimen recovered at Dwārkā (Mate and Ansari 1966: fig. 9.145) (*fig*. 9.1). Several of these have been found at Koṇḍapur in Andhra Pradesh (Dikshit 1952).

Four cylindrical amulets have come from Bhokardan excavation (Deo and Gupte 1974). One of these ascribed to first century BC to third century CE is an interesting piece. It is a beautiful specimen of a collard cylinder with cut granules in relief (Deo and Gupte 1974: fig. 24.157). It is banded at the ends and collars are short, circular and projecting. It is perforated off centre and horizontally (*fig*. 9.2).

Other three specimens from Bhokardan have some common features. They are solid cylinders with raised collars and loops for passing a thread through the perforation. One of these has only one cylinder with double ribbed ends. It is attributed to third century CE (Deo and Gupte 1974: fig. 24.148) (*fig*. 9.4). The other two are cylinders with double ribbed ends. One has incipient (Deo and Gupte 1974: fig. 24.152) collared terminals and the other has ringed (Deo and Gupte 1974: fig. 24.150) terminals with horizontal perforation. These (*fig*. 9.5), fall between the first and the third century CE.

One specimen from Sopārā is made from blue glass. It is a six-sided cylinder datable to the Sātavāhana period, (Bhagawanlal 1883: Pl. XV.3) (*fig*. 9.3). It is undrilled, and like Bhokardan and Ter ribbed specimens, it was probably held by gold catches at either end (*fig*. 8.9).

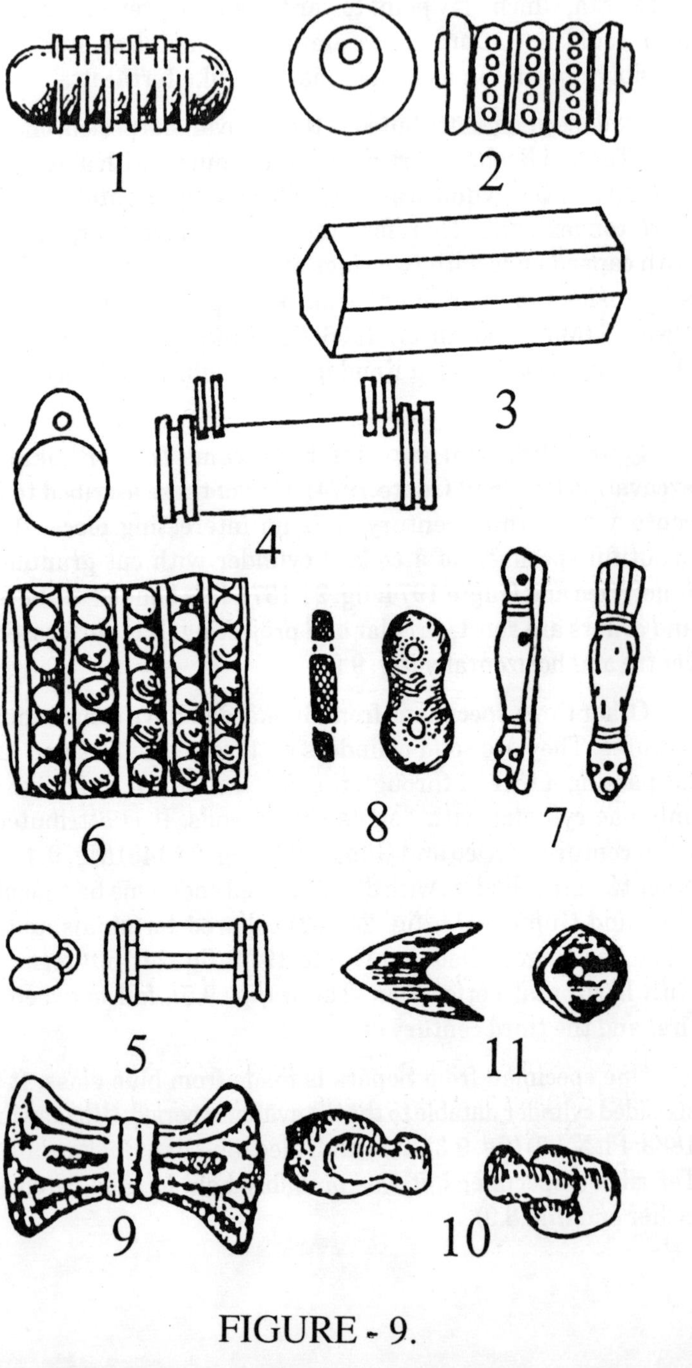

FIGURE - 9.

One circular cylinder of terracotta comes from the Sātavāhana level at Kauṇḍinyapura (Dikshit 1968: Pl.XXXV.3) (*fig*. 9.6). It is decorated with five bands of pellets set within small pelleted zones and pressed from a mould. It is very hard baked, made with well levigated reddish clay, and it has given a lighter yellowish clay wash. Apart from the finds of amulets and pendants from excavations, they have also been found depicted in contemporary sculptures of central and western India. They have been represented invariably as part of the neck ornaments.

Besides large-sized sculptures in which the ornaments are depicted in their natural grace, the coping stones of many a railing at Bhārhut and Pauni are found decorated with garlands and other ornaments, where the principal ornamental motifs are individually portrayed (Barua 1979). Sculptural representations are also found at Sāñcī (Marshall 1955), Amarāvatī (Bachhofer 1954; Barret, 1954; Sivaramamurti 1977), Nāgārjunikoṇḍa (Longhurst 1939), Mādhurī, Sārnāth and caves of western India. These are Hindu, Buddhist or Jaina. It is quite evident that these amulets have some definite religious significance. Most of the depictions in sculptures belong to the Early School of Indian Art, assignable from about the third century BC to the third century CE. Some of the symbols became famous iconographically and attained importance from about the Gupta period. The representations in sculptures clearly indicate the way in which the amulets and pendants have been worn *vis-a-vis* those available from the excavations.

6

Parallels and Interpretations

How far the zeal for symbolic ornaments can carry an artist is evidenced by a pair of strings represented on the outer face of the north gateway of *stūpa* no. 1 (Mode and Chandra 1985: 185). These two strings occur as decorative devices on the face of the gateway along with a number of floral and jewellery strings several of which again can be seen as worn by some of the human figures represented on the same monument. It may not be unreasonable to suggest that actual strings representing these had also been in use.

One of these has as many as eleven symbolic pendants (*fig.* 10.1), while the other has thirteen. These sculptural representations help us not only to study the individual amulets but also to know their general appearance when worn on the body.

Pendants

BUD PENDANTS

Bud pendants are mostly known from Taxilā with the exception of a few from Candravallī and Tripurī. These are made in green glass, carnelian and shell. Taxila specimens belong to *c.* 400-200 BC. The other specimens are known from the Sātavāhana period. Specimens from Maharashtra correspond to those from Candravallī and Tripurī and belong to the same period.

CLUB PENDANTS

Most of them are known from Taxilā and Nagara. These

specimens are made of carnelian, glass, gold and terracotta. These are attributed to *c*. 500-100 BC time bracket.

The specimen from Maharashtra belongs to a much later period. It is attributed to the third century CE. It is quite probable that this shape travelled from Taxila to the Deccan, but it cannot be stated with certainty until and unless more specimens are found from 100 BC to CE 300 level.

CONICAL PENDANTS

Conical pendants occur at Nāgdā, Jokhā, Nagar and Salihundam. These are reported in terracotta. These belongs to 300 BC to CE 400. Nāsik specimen belongs to the lower level of this time bracket, i.e., 400-200 BC. Twenty-four conical pendants in terracotta were found at Veerapuram. They belong to CE 50-100 time bracket (Shastri 1984: Pl. XXIV.6-10).

CRESCENT-SHAPED PENDANTS

Some amulets are crescent-shaped ending in points leaving small gap in between. These are recovered from Koṇḍāpur, Nāgārjunikoṇḍa, Śiśupālgarh, Taxilā and Vaiśālī. These are associated with Kuṣāṇa-Sātavāhana level. The specimens from Maharashtra are also attributed to the Sātavāhana times. In the north and the Deccan these are also portrayed in the art of the Kuṣāṇa-Sātavāhana period.

Evidence of their use as ear-ornaments is available in contemporary sculptures at Amarāvatī (Sivaramamurti 1977: Pl. VII.7, 10) and Mathurā on the sculptures of the Kuṣāṇa period (Agrawala 1939: Pl. IX.21). The famous statue of the so-called priest at Mohenjo-Dāro shows a crescent-shaped fillet on the headband, which may be taken as a pendant (Marshall 1931: Pl. XCVII). This ornament was probably hung at the parting of the hair, as is done today.

At Taxilā (Young 1946: 32, Pl. IX) these were made in gold and terracotta. The gold ones have been decorated with a double border of bosses in repousse arranged crescent-wise around a circular gap. There are two small holes in the gap reinforced by wire-rings in which perhaps hook-like arrangement was made for use as a pendant. Specimens with same width and design along with moulds in terracotta have also been found at Taxila (Marshall 1951-53: II: 461; III Pl. 136.6, 136.4). The finest specimens are known from the Sātavāhana sites. Most of them were prepared from double moulds and profusely decorated. Koṇḍāpur (Dikshit 1952: 24-25, Pl. V.252, VI.262) has yielded them in simple and elaborate decorated types. Simple ones bear several thread marks or ladders ending in a point. The elaborate decorations consist of a series of raised platforms on top, on which there is a rosette with a central knob. The whole area is included in a crescent-shaped platform surrounded by dots, near the margin. The design on Nāgārjunikoṇḍa specimen is similar to that of Bhokardan specimen. At Śiśupālgarh, designs comprise of raised bands at ends, rows of beads, spiral patterns, etc. Here (Lal 1941: Pl. XLVII.13-19) twenty-nine crescent-shaped pendants were associated with second century CE levels. A gold specimen of Kuṣāṇa period has been found in the excavation at Vaiśālī (*IAR*, 1958-9: Pl. X.B).

Crescent-shaped pendants are clearly seen on a ninth-century wall carving in the Tiruttani temple, (Longhust 1924: Pl.XI) Mataṅgeśvara and Tripurāntaka temple at Kāñcī (Rea *ASI*, 1909: Pl. XCVI). This is an integral part of Śiva's *jaṭā-mukuṭa* in the sculptures belonging to different dynastic periods.

In early literature we get references to the various ornaments used at the parting of thc hair (Ganguli 1977-8: 140-9).

DROP PENDANT

Drop pendants are of very wide occurrence and have been reported from Ahicchatra, Arikāmeḍu, Bhir Mouṇḍ, Cambay, Jaṇḍial, Koṇḍāpur, Kośam, Maheśvar, Māskī, Taxilā, Timbarvā (Gujarat) and Vaiśālī, outside Maharashtra.

Drop pendants were made from a variety of materials like

agate, carnelian, chalcedony, faience, gold, granite, glazed quartz, glass, ivory, jasper, lapis-lazuli, shell and terracotta.

Taxilā has yielded specimens in agate, carnelian, gold, lapis-lazuli, shell and terracotta. They are attributed between 500 BC and CE 300.

A gold specimen from Timbarvā (Gujarat) is dated between *c.* CE 100-300.

Drop pendants made in gold have a ringed projection for suspension. They are attributed to *c.* CE 100. At Taxilā, agate and carnelian pendants belong to *c.* 500-300 BC, while those in lapis-lazuli belong to the strata dated between 300 BC and CE 100.

Two drop pendants in green glass are attributed between *c.*400 BC and CE 100. Ghosh (1947) mentions two shell pendants from Taxilā datable from *c.* 400 BC-AD100. Brahmapurī and Sāṁbhar have yielded it in carnelian dated to CE 200-300. Tripurī has yielded it in glass attributed to *c.* CE 100-200. Shell specimen at Māskī belongs to the early centuries of Christian era. Terracotta specimens come from Āhār, Besanagar, Koṇḍāpur, Māskī, Raṅgmahal, Sāṁbhar, Taxilā and Tripurī. These are dated to *c.* 200 BC-CE 300. At Taxilā they occur in *c.* 500 BC to CE 200 bracket.

So, outside Maharashtra drop pendants are dated between *c.* 500 BC and CE 300. In Maharashtra these are attributed to 200 BC to CE 300 bracket.

SPACER PENDANTS

It occurs mostly in central India and the Deccan and is made in terracotta. It is predominantly reported from Sātavāhana sites. They are in the form of an ornamental devise in the shape of horizontal and vertical flutings or ribbings at top and an elongated tapering body below. This type occurs at Koṇḍāpur, Taxilā, Tripurī and Ujjain.

Another popular type consists of a pillar-like pendant with a fluted device at top and elongated tapering body below with two perforations. These are mostly made from double moulds and decorated in different designs. Koṇḍāpur (Dikshit 1954) has the lower part decorated with a fluted *āmalaka* or clustered beads. They occur also at Ujjain. At Tripurī (Dikshit 1952) they are made from moulds. They consist of three unequal parts divided by short zonal bands near the ends and usual ribbing on the top. The underside is flat and each one has lateral perforations decorated with dots and pellets, and some are even painted.

A rare specimen from Koṇḍāpur appears to have been made in imitation of some leaves and served the function of a spacer in between two beads. The top hole shows that it may have been used as a pendant also (Dikshit 1954: Pl. V.224).

AMULETS

<table>
<tr><td colspan="6">Amulets with animals and their components representation</td></tr>
<tr><td colspan="2">Bull Amulets</td><td colspan="2">Fish Amulets</td><td colspan="2">Lion Amulets</td></tr>
<tr><td colspan="2">Makara Amulets</td><td colspan="2">Claw Amulets</td><td colspan="2">Tortoise Amulets</td></tr>
<tr><td colspan="6">Amulets with artifactual representation</td></tr>
<tr><td colspan="6">Dagger Amulets</td></tr>
<tr><td colspan="6">Amulets with human body and its components as Amulets</td></tr>
<tr><td colspan="3">Eye Beads</td><td colspan="3">Yakṣa Amulets</td></tr>
<tr><td colspan="3">Human-figure Amulets</td><td colspan="3">Tooth Amulets</td></tr>
<tr><td colspan="6">Amulets with religious symbols</td></tr>
<tr><td colspan="2">Casket Amulets</td><td colspan="2">Triratna Amulets</td><td colspan="2">Stūpa Amulets,</td></tr>
<tr><td colspan="3">Conch-shell Amulets</td><td colspan="3">Nandīpada Amulets</td></tr>
<tr><td colspan="3">Pīpal-leaf Amulets</td><td colspan="3">Heart-shaped Amulets</td></tr>
<tr><td colspan="6">Miscellaneous</td></tr>
<tr><td colspan="6">Cylindrical Amulets (Tāveez),</td></tr>
</table>

Amulets with animals and their components representation

BULL AMULETS

It is a popular motif reported from a number of sites in India. It is sacred to both the Hindus and the Buddhists. For Buddhists, it stands for asterism Taurus on which the Buddha was born. It is well-known to the Brāhmaṇic faith as the vehicle of Śiva, and it was always depicted in theromorphic form. Nandī amulets at Taxilā (Beck 1941: 18, Pl. VII-9) and Rairh (Puri: Pl. XVI.7) are hand-made with humps depicted realistically. They are datable between *c.* 300 and 200 BC. A number of bull amulets in seated posture are known from Koṇḍāpur (Dikshit 1952) and Vaiśālī (Deva and Mishra 1961).

The similarity of representation of bull amulets at many places suggests their popular use during the early centuries of the Christian era. A crystal bull amulet is recovered from Kośam (Dikshit 1954).

A carnelian bull amulet from the Bhir Mouṇḍ is dated to third century BC (Beck 1941: Pl. VII.9). This specimen has a transverse hole across and the figure hangs by its tail and the hind parts of the body. Another carnelian specimen was unearthed at Kauśāṁbī excavations. At Koṇḍāpur, some of them show the humped bull in a siting posture with its face turned to one side. By far the most common form seems to be the animal-facing front.

Two bull-shaped amulets have been found from excavations at Vaiśālī, in gold with tabular attachments at the back. These are assigned to the Kuṣāṇa-Gupta period.

The bull stands for virility and power from the Ṛgvedic time, and in the Buddhist tradition it represents the asterism on which the Buddha was born. The amulets take different shapes, the earlier ones being in semi-precious stones; but later, popularity for comparatively larger specimen is evidenced by numerous specimens encountered at Sātavāhana sites in the Deccan. On these sites, the bull assumes larger dimensions in a crude material, such as terracotta. It is likely that these amulets represent Nandī, the well-known *vāhana* of Śiva.

CLAW AND TOOTH AMULETS

The claws have a hoary antiquity in India and they are still prevalent. These have long been known to possess talismanic value. They are known from Amrelī, Nāgdā, Sāṁbhar and Taxilā made in bone, chalcedony, faience, ivory, marble, shell and terracotta.

An early gold sheath of tooth amulet at Taxilā (Marshall 1951-53 II: 504-5; III Pl. 142.e; 191.o; Beck, 1941: Pl. IV.17) has been decorated with fine filigree work in criss-cross pattern. This is attributed to *c*. 600-500 BC bracket. While another has a lead core with similar thin sheath of gold at the point. On the front the gold is decorated with a granulated design of small hexagons enclosed in beaded borders. This is attributed to the *c*. 300 BC.

Nāgdā has yielded one from *c*. 200-100 BC level, in chalcedony. Sirkap (Marshall 1951-53 II: 665; III: Pl. 199.17) has yielded one in bone or ivory in the form of crude buckranium consisting of a pair of animal teeth bound up with strips of copper. Sāṁbhar has also yielded one. One of them at Amrelī (Rao: Pl. XLI.5) is in the shape of a tiger's nail decorated with pallets in relief.

These are attributed between *c*. CE 200-300 whereas specimens in Maharashtra belong to 200 BC to CE 100 level. Marshall aptly infers that these are credited with specific apotropaic and other powers (Marshall 1951-3: II 665). The literary tradition for the wearing of the tiger claws can be traced to the period of *Harṣavardhana* and is mentioned in many later works. The *Harṣacarita* (Agrawala 1969: 92) mentions that the necks of children were decorated with rows of claws. Bāṇa also refers to this practice in *Kādambarī* (Kadambari, Nirnayasagar: 420). A tenth-century work *Vikramāṅkadeva Carita* of Bilhana refers to buds of tiger claws around the neck (Canto 3.13).

Even a late work like *Līlācarita* dated to the thirteenth century CE mentions tiger claws as an ornament (Nene {ed.}: 178). Through the literary tradition is at present limited to seventh century CE onwards, the ornament seems to have gained popularity during the Gupta period. The ornament is distinctly carved on many a Gupta sculptures as well as in bronze images (Coomaraswamy 1980: Pl. XLVI.175). — Gaṇa from Khoh in the Prince of Wales Museum, Bombay bears tiger's tooth pendant around his neck (*fig.* 10.2). This ornament is a peculiar feature on images of Kārttikeya, Kṛṣṇa, Balarāma, etc., amongst Brāhmaṇical images and those of Mañjuśrī and others in the Buddhist pantheon. The human tooth as an amulet is rarely used except for sorcery in India. Pliny mentions the various uses to which different teeth are used.

FISH AMULETS

Like tortoise, another aquatic being well represented is fish. Only a few fish amulets have been found and most of them are reported from north India (Dikshit 1954), excepting a few at Taxila, Tripurī and Ujjain.

Tripurī (Dikshit 1952: 105, Pl. XXXIX.7) has yielded one in copper, designed in the shape of double-fish, datable to *c.* 400-300 BC. Fish depicted as amulet at Taxilā (Marshall 1951-3: II, 558; III, Pl. 179f) is made in copper and consists of a pair of them hanging side by side on a tiny string. A few fish-shaped amulets have come from Kośam (Dikshit 1952). One made of banded agate, and another of glazed quartz, are available in the Allahabad Museum. Two quartz beads of this category from Kośam are in the Bhārat Kalā Bhavan, Vārāṇasī. One tiny carnelian specimen has come from Mādhurī. A specimen of jade is known from Rajasthan. Most of these are without stratigraphical context. Fish-shaped amulet is known from Yeraṇḍavaṇe. This microlithic specimen has a pit for the point of the drill (Kosambi 1962: 151) (*fig.* 10.3).

A pair of fish is one of the *aṣṭamaṅgala*s — eight auspicious signs — of the Jaina ideology (Jain 1947: 236) and is of well-known amuletic value. The fishes are depicted in both the garlands represented at Sāñcī, and curiously copper pendants of this shape are known from actual specimens.

Fish is also found in girdles of gold from Taxilā (Marshall 1951-3: II 630) attributable to *c.* 100 CE. They consist of three rows of fishes joined by clasps. Another specimen from Taxilā dated in the Śaka-Pārthian period shows two fishes in union, suspended by a ring loop (Marshall 1951-3: II 581; Pl. 172.h).

Indian literature is replete with references to the fish described as the emblem on the banner of the God of Love. Its shape is compared with the eyes of a woman. In historic times, the fish has been the symbol of several dynasties like Pāṇḍyas, Saindhavas, etc. Fish is considered as a symbol of fertility. In about the fifth centuty CE Kālidāsa mentions the fish emblem as a part of the girdle worn by court ladies (*Kumārasambhava*, 9.26). The earliest stratified specimen is from Mathurā, associated with Mauryan layers (*IAR*, 1975-6: 53-5). A large number of these are reported from Ahicchatra attributed to first-second century CE (Dikshit 1952: Pl. XII.72), Tripurī (Dikshit 1952), and Koṇḍāpur specimens are dated to (Dikshit 1954: Pl. II.61) *c.* first century CE.

In the *Bṛhat-Kalpa-Sūtra-Bhāṣya* (Jain 1947: 236) the fish is considered to be an auspicious symbol. The *Vāsudevahiṇḍi*, a fourth and fifth-century CE work, mentions an amulet called *Macchapada* (Jamkhedkar 1984).

LION AMULETS

Lion occupies a very prominent place as an amuletic symbol. Not only does it symbolise power, but is sacred to the Buddhists as it represents the Buddha, the 'lion of the Śākya race'. All the amulets represent the full figure of the animal (Dikshit 1954: 94). Taxilā (Beck 1941: Pl. VII.3, 4, 5, 6, 7) has yielded the best of them in addition to other sites such as Besanagar and Saṁbhar. These are dated between first century BC and first century CE. At Taxilā they are made in glazed quartz, carnelian, lapis-lazuli and garnet. One of them at Sāṁbhar (Sahni : Pl. XV.j) is in green glazed faience representing a couchant lion.

Lion amulets differ from region to region in respect of their typology. The specimens at Taxilā show the full figure of the lion with rounded back. Some specimens have their terminals ending in a series of scales all over the body; but the simplification of this is seen in the crystal specimen from Nāsik. Siṁha-kuṇḍala's are seen on the figures of Bodhisattva from Shabhazgarhi (Musee Guimet, Paris) and Maitreya from Pakistan (Ingholt 1957 Pl. 293) (*fig*. 10.4-10.5)

In the *Kunāla Jātaka* (No. 536) a queen is described as wearing earrings of the shape of lions head. This meager literary evidence is compensated by a large number of actual specimens found at a number of sites in India.

The workmanship of the Taxilā specimens appears to be rather inferior in quality, but the north Indian amulets aim at a faithful reproduction of the natural form and show a superior technique in their manufacture.

The Indian specimens are generally dated between the third century BC and second century CE. Specimens from Maharashtra belong to the Sātavāhana period.

MAKARA AMULET

Outside Maharashtra, *makara* has been reported from Koṇḍāpur, in Andhra. Here (Dikshit 1952: PL. V.2, 5) it consists of two pieces, one face has *makara* and other is in the form of a pillar like strut made in double mould. It is attributed to the Sātavāhana period. One of agate, somewhat less defined, was found in the excavation at Rājghāṭ, Vārāṇasī (Dikshit 1954).

Among the major groups of animals represented in Indian art, the *makaras* are depicted on pottery, sculptures, amulets and terracotta plaques. The important ancient sites yielding such depictions are Hastināpura, Kauśāmbī, Kumrahāra, Rājghāṭ and Vaiśālī in the Gaṅgā valley. Nāgārjunīkoṇḍā, Rājghāṭ and Hastināpura depiction is on a spout, which bears at the luting

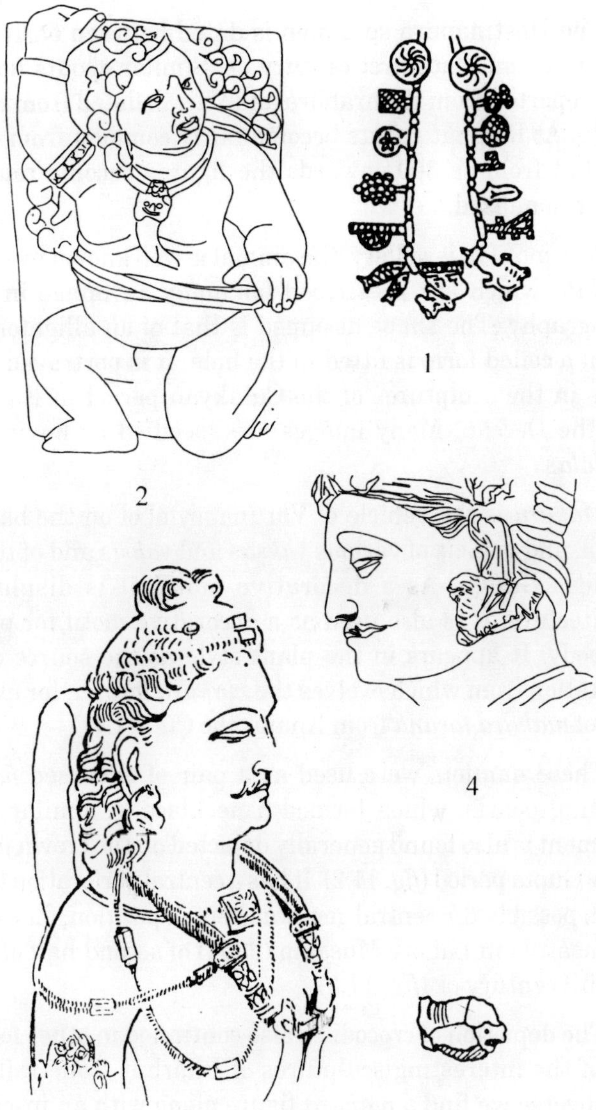

FIGURE - 10.

point a decorative mould design of a *makara-mukha*. The earliest Rājghāṭ specimen is dated from second century BC to the beginning of the Christian era.

The Hastināpura specimen is dated between early second century BC and late first century CE. Similar spouts have also been reported from Kumrahāra and Vaiśālī dated from *c*. CE 100 to 300. At Rājghāṭ spouts become fairly common from CE 0 to 300, but from CE 300 onwards the figures become rough and conventionalised.

As a motif in jewellery, the animal is well known by *makara-kuṇḍala* which are prescribed for many an image in Indian iconography. The shape assumed is that of an alligator whose tail in a coiled form is fitted in the hole. It is portrayed several times in the sculptures of the Cālukyan period in Karnataka and the Deccan. Many images are specified as having these *kuṇḍala*s.

Makara is the vehicle of Varuṇa, symbol on the banner of Kāma, and vehicle of various *yakṣa*s and *yakṣī*s and of the river goddess Gaṅgā. As a decorative motif, it is displayed in architecture. It is also used as a decorative motif for painting the body. It appears in the plant style as the source of lotus vegetation from which evolves the *makara toraṇa*, for example, part of *makara toraṇa* from Khajurāho (*fig*. 11.1).

These amulets were used as a pair of addorsed *makara*s emitting pearls, which formed a necklace. A similar type of ornament is also found generally depicted on the crown in vogue in the Gupta period (*fig*. 11.2). It has a central perforation through which possibly the central gem was kept in position, for example, Bodhisattva in Lahore Museum (2354) of second half of second or third century CE (*fig*. 11.3).

The depiction of crocodiles also continued in other forms. In one of the interesting sculptures of Bhārhut stone railing, on the obverse we find a *makara* figure along with an inscription. *Aṅga-vijjā* mentions *makarikā* as an ornament used by men and women.

In Gāndhāra period the figures of Maitreya and Avalokiteśvara have a large number of amulets in a string (*fig*. 11.4). The *makarikā* ornaments is profusely used (Sharma 1994). The necklace of the Lahore Maitreya shows a central jewel with two *makarikā*s by their side bending in 'hockey stick' loops, which in turn encase a multi-threaded cluster of pearl necklaces. This form of *makarikā* ornament is quite common. *Makarikā* is seen on the Visnu torso also (Sharma 1994: Pl. XXXII) (*fig*. 11.5).

TORTOISE AMULETS

Tortoise-shaped amulets are very common all over India. It has a timeworn antiquity. In the historic times it is reported from many sites like, Amrelī, Maskī, Sāṁbhar, Taxilā, Ujjain. Some unstratified specimens have been recovered from Aundh, Bālāpur, Manikyāla, Sahri-Bahol. In the Gangetic valley a few sites are Ahicchatra, Kośam, Mādhurī, Paṭnā and Rājghāṭ. A great variety of material is used such as copper, garnet, agate, carnelian, chalcedony, crystal, mother-of-pearl, malachite, faience, shell and terracotta. In central and western India most of them are prepared of faience and shell. The great diversity of material talks a ton about its popularity. Tortoise amulet in terracotta is reported from Ujjain (Thapar 1967: 110; Banerjee 1954: Pl. V-7; Dikshit 1968: 97). Like Ter, Sambhar (Sahni: 39, Pl. XV.K) has also yielded one in green glazed faience. Many shell amulets have been found in the private collection from Ter.

Six tortoise amulets have been reported at Taxilā (Marshall 1951-3: II 748). Five are illustrated by Beck, (Beck 1941: Pl. VII.22-26). These are made of various materials like garnet, faience, glazed quartz and mother-of-pearl. One each of garnet and mother-of-pearl comes from Dharmarājika *stūpa* (Beck 1941: Pl. VII.25, 26) datable to the first century BC. Rest of the specimens are from Sirkāp, made of glazed quartz, green faience and malachite (Beck 1941: Pl. VII.22, 23, 24; Dikshit 1968: 97). These are dated to first century CE. Identical specimen has come from a megalithic burial at Rāipur, near Nāgpur (Deglurkar and Lad 1992).

Kośam has given a terracotta specimen which is attributed to the first century CE. Dikshit, (Dikshit 1954) states six tortoise amulets from Kośam. The materials used are chalcedony, agate, rock crystal, banded agate and carnelian.

Two carnelian tortoise amulets are recovered from Kumrahāra. Excavation at Rājghāṭ has yielded two tortoise amulets in terracotta. Mādhurī contributed a carnelian amulet. One specimen is reported from Ahicchatra in garnet (Dikshit 1952: 48). In the early historic period it appears on punch-marked coins (Allan 1936). Among the Jainas it serves as the *lāñchaṇā* of Sāntīnatha, Arā and Muni Suvrata, the sixteenth, eighteenth and twentieth *tīrthaṁkaras* respectively (Fergusson and Burgess 1880). Among the subsidiary *yakṣas* tortoise is the vehicle of Yakṣa Ajita, of the ninth *tīrthaṁkara* Suvidhi; of *yakṣa kinnara* of the fifteenth *tīrthaṁkara* Dharma and of *pārśva yakṣa* Dharaṇendra. A sandstone *yakṣa* figure from Nachna wears a tortoise in his necklace. This figure belongs to the sixth/seventh century CE (*fig*. 11.6). From the earliest time Kāśyapa is identified with the sun, and the amulets and charms handled by them are said to be powerful (Max Müller, 1897: 403). In the *Mahābhārata* it is associated with wisdom and longevity. The *Bṛhat-saṁhitā* of Varāha states that the king should keep a tortoise as an auspicious sign (*Mbh*, Vanaparva, Ch.149; *Bṛhat-saṁhitā*, LXIV.3).

Though tortoise is a favourite animal in sculptural depictions of the early school of Indian art, it assumes importance only from the Gupta period (Agrawala 1947: 8). It starts occupying the front doorway of the temple as the vehicle of Yamunā from this time (Agrawala 1947: Pl. XVII.V) and continues to gain added significance in the later historic period. It is one of the incarnations of Viṣṇu.

Pottery models were in vogue at the Indus sites (Vats 1952: 303). A stone model has been recovered from the excavation at Balathal, Rajasthan, in Chalcolithic period (Mishra, V. N. *et al*. 1995).

In Indian temples the representation of the tortoise in the *maṇḍapa* of Śaiva and Vaiṣṇava temples is a common sight. These amulets were no doubt used as symbols of longevity and other sacred associations. It is however, interesting to observe that in some medieval (eleveenth century CE) images of Kārttikeya from Orissa, the tortoise pendant is displayed prominently (Kramrisch 1933: Pl. 9,10). The photograph of an image of Kārttikeya from the Kedārnāth Temple at Bhubaneśvara in the Nagpur Museum shows a tortoise in the necklace. In the temples of medieval period tortoise is very often depicted on the *dvāra-śākhā* as the *vāhana* of Yamunā or as the Matsya *avatāra* of Viṣṇu.

In medieval times we get representations in metal as at Ujjain (*IAR*, 1959-60: Pl. CVII). From the point of view of their typology it appears that these amulets were generally flat and their snouts less pronounced. They are hung by their neck. In the Gangetic Valley, this snout is very prominent and specimens were occasionally provided with pedestals.

From the above description it is clear that this type of amulet has been found to be more popular and widely used during the period 200 BC-CE 200. However, in Maharashtra from Chalcolithic period it prevails till Sātavāhana period. Quite significantly tortoise as an iconographic concept does not seem to have been reported after the second century CE. It completely goes out of fashion after the third century CE. A male figure in a sitting posture from Paiṭhan has a tortoise pendant or rather a spacer in his necklace (Dhavalikar 1975-6: Pl. XXIV.10).

A female figure (Dhavalikar 1975-6: Pl. XXIV.6) again from Paiṭhan consists of a tortoise amulet in the shortest necklace.

Amulets with artifactual representation

DAGGER AMULETS

A large number of amulets take the shape of a dagger. These are by far the largest among the specimens recovered so far. This is the shape of a weapon-like motif found both in plain and decorated forms. Many early historic sites have yielded them in agate, bone, carnelian, chalcedony, copper, faience, glass, ivory, lapis-lazuli, shell and terracotta.

Dagger amulets seem to have been more popular during *c.* 300 BC-CE 300 at sites like Ahicchatra, Koṇḍāpur, Māskī Maheśvar, Taxilā, Tripurī, Arikāmeḍu, Kauśāmbī and Vaiśālī.

Dagger pendants in agate, carnelian and faience have been reported from Taxilā in horizons belonging to the fourth and third century BC.

The earliest dagger of a long leaf pattern, triangular in section, coming from Taxila is made of agate and is dated to the fourth century BC. A similar one in carnelian is dated to third century BC. A broad blade and a beaded top characterise it. One in ivory is decorated on the blade-side with parallel lines and a circle, and another one, in bone, has decoration made on the entire body with a perforation made on the handle. At Sirkāp, bone dagger amulets were found decorated with incised lines on handle and blades, datable to *c.* CE 100. Taxila has thus yielded both plain and decorated specimens made in agate, carnelian, bone, glass and ivory. A similar one at Hathial, dated *c.* CE 100-300 has two small holes near the blade and incised parallel lines on hilt and blade (*IAR*, 1958-9: pl. LX.4).

At Śrāvastī, dagger-shaped pendants have a triangular cross-section. A pair of carnelian specimens is dated about mid-third century BC-150 BC. In the excavation at Vaiśālī (Deva and Mishra 1961: Pl. XXIX-B.15) several pendants of identical shape occur in the Mauryan stratum. The dagger assumes different shapes with a curved blade of long-tapering point in the Sātavāhana period in the Deccan. In the south, these are somewhat rare. One in lapis-lazuli and another one in faience are known from Koṇḍāpur (Dikshit 1954: Pl. II, 3-4, 10). One ivory dagger amulet from Ujjain (*ARADGS*, 1938-9: Pl. XXV.C) is decorated with pellets over the blade and has two perforations at the joint of the blade and the hilt. One of them, at Jokhā (Mehta & Chowdhary 1971: 51, fig. 22.5; Pl. VII.A), is made of a splinter of a long bone. It is

FIGURE - 11.

attributed to *c*. 500-300 BC. It is a small dagger with horizontal lines and dots in rows of three and two. On terracotta figurines from Ahicchatra three symbols are worn in the long-necklace namely a dagger on the left, *śrīvatsa* in the centre and on the right a *vajra* with a pointed angle (Agrawala 1947: fig. 1.1). A similar figure has come from Paunī (*fig*. 12.7) Terracotta figures from Ahicchatrā (*fig*. 12.1) depict many religious symbols as their hair-dress. This type of necklace is found on all the female figures of the *mithuna* sub-types, and it is a regular feature on the archaic terracottas of the modelled-*cum*-moulded variety from Mathurā, belonging to the Śuṅga period.

The dagger in an elongated form, like a leaf with prominent median, however, appears to be the most patent shape favoured by the Indians in all periods. The specimens are generally horizontally perforated at the top, but occasionally, they occur with two perforations intended as spacers. From the Harappan times they appear as the terminals in many a necklace. The type seems to have been a favourite one from about fourth century BC to first century CE. A large number of similar daggers are knows in shell from Māskī (*ANADNA*: 1935-6). The dagger assumes a leaf-shaped outline with a constricted centre, in the Kuṣāṇa-Gupta specimens at Vaiśālī (*IAR*, 1958-9: pl. XI.A). Here, silver amulets are provides with a spiral tenon and are looped with tubular holes. On account of the efficacy of the shape, the dagger continues in some form or the other even during the Muslim-Marāṭhā period. A very late dagger in carnelian from Maheśvar (Sankalia, *et al.* 1958: fig. 102.18) is dated to the Muslim-Marāṭhā period.

Garlands with daggers are described as *aśi-mallikā* in the *Aṅga-Vijjā* (Punyavijaya 1957: 163-4).

Human body and its components represented as amulets

EYE BEADS

Eye beads from Maharashtra have several parallels from Taxilā,

Sirkāp, Kauśāmbī, Śrāvastī, Ujjain, Rājghāṭ, Ahicchatra and Koṇḍāpur. These specimens are made in glass. Terracotta eye bead similar to Brahmapurī specimen has been reported at Besanagar. These belong to fifth century BC to second century CE time bracket. The eye beads from Maharashtra are attributed to the upper level of this time bracket. Associated with the concept of 'Evil Eye', they have a wide provenance.

HUMAN-SHAPED AMULETS

This type is known from Taxilā and Ujjain. One of them, in gold, comes from Ujjain datable to *c*. 500-200 BC (*IAR*, 1957-8: 36). Another, in chalcedony, occurs at Taxilā datable to *c*. 300-200 BC (Beck 1941: Pl. VII.I) representing a headless human figure. A rare one at Taxilā, datable to *c*. CE 100, is in ivory adorned on either side with a bearded Greek head of Socrates-type philosopher (Marshall 1951-3: II, 666: III, Pl. 203).

A group of female figurines occur at a number of sites in north and north-western India (Dhavalikar 1965: 533-40). They are made in shell, bone and ivory. They represent an outline of human figures with decorations comprising of several incised circles or dots on the outer surface all over. They occur in the time span of *c*.200 BC-CE 200 at Nāgdā, (*IAR*, 1955-6: 14, Pl. XXIV.B), Prabhās Pāṭan (*IAR*, 1956-7: Pl. XVIII.B.5), Taxilā (Marshall 1951-3, II; 654-5; III, Pl. 199.12; *IAR*, 1956-7: 36), Ujjain (*IAR*, 1956-7: 23), Chandraketugarh (*IAR*,: 1957-8), Sonepur (*IAR*: 1956-7), Śrāvastī (*IAR*: 1958-9), Somanāth (Sankalia, *et al*. 1960: 373), Singh Bhagwānpur (*IAR*: 1980-1) and Sanghol (*IAR*: 1987-8).

The human body is very rarely portrayed in Indian amulets Early figures are comparatively rare. The excavations at Mohenjo-Dāro (Mackey 1938: II, 523; Pl. LXXXII.7) have yielded in faience a ram-headed human figure with Mongoloid features. This is described as an amulet. Ahicchatra (Dikshit 1952: fig. 4.83) has given a small serpentine amulet showing a pregnant woman in a squatting posture with bent legs, probably used as a charm against difficult labour. It may be attributed to the Śuṅga period. At Vaiśālī (*IAR*, 1958: Pl. X.B) a standing male figure in gold repousse work was found fitted with hallow tubes at the back. This probably was used as a pendant. It is attributable to the Kuṣāṇa period.

At Ahicchatra a tiny copper-bead (Dikshit 1952: Pl. XII.B; fig. 6.129) represents a human figure. It has its legs spread wide apart and the feet are joined together. The *Aṅga-vijjā* describes necklace decorated with three goblins and *vidyādharas*, as constituent part. Among the Gāndhāra sculptures (Agrawala 1947: Pl. LXIV 301) we find that the figure of Maitreya is often represented as wearing a necklace in which the central gem is supported by winged females which seems to corroborate the description of the *Aṅga-vijjā* (*fig*. 12.2).

These figures are earlier, while at Nevāsā they belong to early Christian era, like Sanghol specimen.

Amulets with religious symbols

CONCH-SHELL AMULET

Shell used as an amulet is evidenced as far back as the period of the *Atharvaveda* (Privrajak 1941). One specimen has been reported from Sanghol datable to the Kuṣāṇa period (*IAR*, 1987-8). Another one comes from Dwārkā ascribed to the medieval period (Ansari and Mate 1966).

Several terracotta specimens of Sātavāhana date occur at Koṇḍāpur. A gold bead, shaped like a shell, is known from Bhītā. It is dated to Kuṣāṇa-Gupta period. A copper specimen from Ahicchatra is attributed to CE 800-1100.

Real conches were used as amulets from the Harappan times. A specimen from Ujjain belongs to the period 500-200 BC. As an amulet, the conch is used either by perforating the shell for stringing or by making amulets of diverse materials carved in imitation of the conch. One specimen made in coral has been recovered form the *vajrāsana* at Mahābodhi (Cunningham 1892: Pl. XXII.28). Koṇḍāpur has yielded several terracotta specimens dated to the Sātavāhana period (Dikshit 1952: fig.V.241). A gold specimen is known from Bhītā attributed to Kuṣāṇa-Gupta period (*ARASI*, 1911-12: Pl. XXXII.6). At Ahicchatra a copper specimen is attributed to CE 800-1100 (Dikshit 1952: Pl. XIII.B.128).

A unique shell pendant in *śaṅkha* from Saṅghol has an inverted bell-shaped cover soldered to fit in for hanging. It belongs to the Kuṣāṇa period (*IAR*, 1987-8). To use conch-shells as amulets, their tops were either ground or pierced or it was capped with metal cap. Mohenjo-Dāro has yielded seven specimens (Mackey 1938: Pl. CXl.65, 70, 83). A specimen from Ujjain belongs to the CE 500-200 bracket (Banerjee 1959: Pl. V.30). Another is known from Brahmagirī (Wheeler 1947).

From the *Mahābhārata*, we learn about the sacred association of shell in coronation ceremonies and as an object of veneration (*Mbh*, Droṇaparvan, 82,20). The Buddhist literature includes *śaṅkha* among the auspicious objects (*Mahāvaṁsa*, XI.30-31; *Dīpavaṁsa*, XI.32-3; Cowell and Neil (ed.), *Divyāvadāna*, 116.8). Śaṅkha was also used in *Dhammila* type hair style as seen in a Surasundari image from Bijamandala excavation at Khajurāho and kept in Jardin Open Air Museum (*fig.* 12.3) (acc no. Rh8). In the Gupta period, the *śaṅkha* was reckoned as a sign of regality (*Raghuvaṁśa*, IX.3), and the depicting/carving of a conch on the door was held in great veneration (*Meghadūtam*, II.20).

The sounding of a conch foretold the beginning of a war, and also the victory (*Meghadūtam*, I.63). As an auspicious symbol is it represented in many sculptures and paintings (Yazdani 1931-55: II, Pl. XLVII). Varāhamihira (CE 550) classifies the conch-shell as one of the twenty-two gems (*Bṛhatsaṁhitā*, LXXX.5). In the *Harṣacarita*, elephants are stated to have been decorated with *śaṅkha* motifs (Agrawala 1953: 40). *Rājataraṅgiṇī* (Stein (ed.), 1741:VIII) mentions *Śaṅkhakṛti-ratna-kuṇḍala*s.

HEART-SHAPED AMULET

A bone specimen comes from Taxilā made in a cloisonné-like technique. It is divided into round cloisonné's in each of, which is a minute disc of mica fixed into a bed of lack, and once probably backed by some colour.

NANDĪPADA AMULET

As stated earlier (fifth chapter), the *nandīpada* or taurine symbol is commonly associated with Śiva worship but was specially adopted by the Buddhists as a symbol of their trinity. Both *triratna* and *nandīpada* are indistinguishable in their main features and are similar in shape as long as they appear as amulets.

Not many amulets of this shape have been reported so far. Taxilā (Beck 1941: Pl. III.19) has yielded this amulet in agate. It is datable to the Mauryan period. A few of them are reported from Koṇḍāpur (Dikshit 1954: Pl. V.20) made in terracotta. The Bhokardan specimen is also made by pressing two decorated pieces together with a small stick in between. This stick helped in creating a horizontal perforation.

PĪPAL LEAF AMULET

Leaf-shaped amulet is a favourite design among the Buddhists as the Buddha attends enlightenment under a *pīpal* tree. These are reported in large numbers during *c.* 200 BC-CE 200 made in copper, chalcedony, glazed quartz, gold, shell, iron and terracotta.

Outside Maharashtra, these are reported from Amrelī, Koṇḍāpur, Taxilā and Tripurī.

Tripurī has yielded this motif in shell in complete form with perforated top. It is datable between *c.* 300-200 BC (Dikshit 1952: Pl. XXXII. B, fig. 36, 47, 51). Similar amulets in gold also come from Taxilā. At Koṇḍapur (Dikshit 1952: Pl. II.102, V.225) and Tripurī terracotta specimens are decorated in high relief with a flat underside.

At Koṇḍapur, some of them are also made in chalcedony with fine carving and a medial ridge at centre forming the stem of leaf. Sirkap (Beck 1941: Pl. V.23, 24; VIII.22) has yielded them in glazed quartz and shell. Amrelī (Rao 1966: Pl. XLI.7, 9, 11)

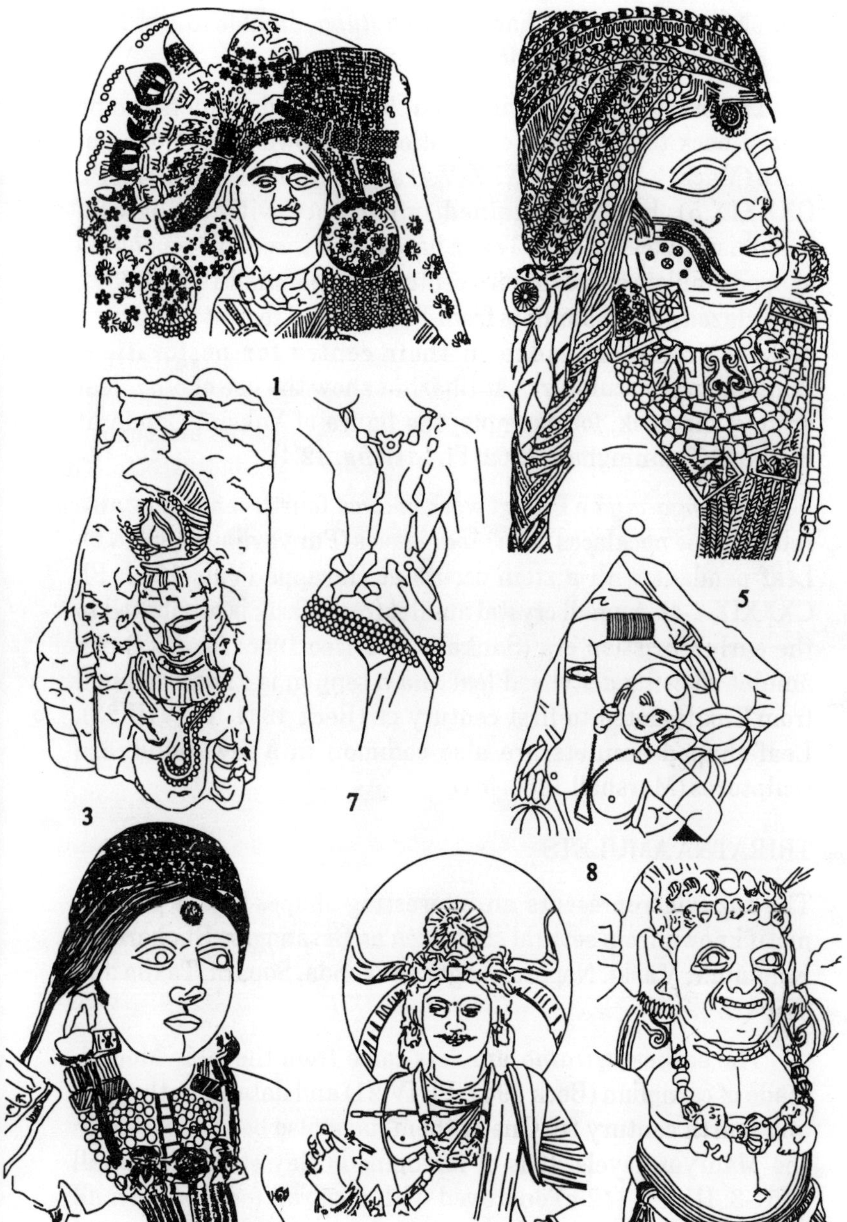

FIGURE - 12.

has given them in terracotta datable to *c.* CE 200-300. A copper leaf-shaped amulet at Dharmarājika *stūpa*, datable to *c.* CE 500, has been decorated with dots.

The practice of preparing *pīpal* leaf-shaped amulets can be traced back to the Indus civilisation as known from Mohenjo-Dāro (Mackey 1938: Pl. CXXXIV.4) and Harappā (Vats 1940: Pl. CXXXIX.5), but these gained importance with the rise of Buddhism. Excavation at Taxilā has yielded three gold *pīpal* leaf-shaped amulets dated to third century BC (Marshall 1951-3: 631). Two glazed quartz amulets from Taxilā dated to first century CE have a prominent ridge in their centre for perforation. Contemporary sculptures at Bhārhut show the use of *pīpal* leaf around the neck; for example, the figure of Yakṣiṇī Candā at Bhārhut (Cunningham 1962: Pl. LII) (*fig.* 12.4).

The *Aṅga-vijjā* a Prākr̥t work of *circa* fourth century CE also refers to the necklaces with *pīpal* leaves (Punyavijaya 1957: 71). Leaf pendant with a stem occurs at Harappā (Vats 1940: Pl. CXXXIX.3-4). A small crystal amulet from Nāsik is attributed to the early Christian era (Sankalia and Deo 1955: fig. 45.7). An amulet showing a stylised leaf and a tennon is known in shell from Taxilā dated to first century CE (Beck 1941: Pl. VIII.23). Leaf-shaped amulets are also common in a few Gāndhāra sculptures (Marshall 1960: 161).

TRIRATNA AMULETS

The *triratna* represents an interesting shape. It is a popular motif known from several sites such as Besanagar, Bhokardan, Koṇḍāpur, Māskī, Nagara, Nāgārjunikoṇḍa, Sopārā, Taxilā and Tripurī.

The earliest *triratna* amulets come from the Bhir Mouṇḍ, made of carnelian (Beck 1941: Pl. IV.21) and datable to the fifth and fourth century BC. One of them have also been reported in the Mauryan levels. It is of ferruginous clay stone (Marshall 1951-3: III, Pl. 142.n) engraved with a spirali form pattern all over its front surface. It has a plain flat back. Two others come from Dharmarājika *stūpa* made of shell and garnet (Beck 1941:

Pl. IV.21; Marshall 1951-3: Pl. 142.m). These are attributed to the first century BC. A number of specimens come from Sirkāp. These are made of carnelian, (Beck 1941: Pl. IV.22) serpentine (Beck 1941: Pl. I.25), terracotta and ivory (Beck 1941: pl. X.14) belonging to the first century CE. The shape is repeated amongst the beads from the reliquary of the Piprāwā *stūpa* (Subbarao 1953: fig. 30). These are also known from the Manikyāla *stūpa* (*JRAS*, 1898: 869-70) and from Buddha Gayā (Cunningham 1892: Pl. XXII.28). The former is in carnelian and the latter in mother-of-pearl. The exact date of a specimen from Lauriyā Nandangarh (*ARASI*, 1934-5: Pl.XXII.m) is not known. A jasper *triratna* amulet was found at Tripurī (Mackey 1938: 643) amongst stratified deposits, dated to *c.* second century CE. Koṇḍāpur (Dikshit 1952: Pl. I.17) has also yielded carnelian amulet of *triratna* shape and probably belong to the same period, i.e., second century CE. There are a number of specimens, mostly in carnelian, from Kauśāmbī and Rājghāṭ, in Allahabad Museum.

Māskī and Koṇḍāpur have yielded the finest specimens (Dikshit 1952). Two *triratna* amulets made in amethyst and beryl are known from Sopārā *stūpa* (Bhagawanlal 1885: 273). Nagara (Mehta 1968: fig. 61.B, 143) has yielded a terracotta specimen. At Nāgārjunikoṇḍa, a few coral amulets come from levels of the early Christian era (Sankalia, *et al.*, 371-2). *Triratna* amulet has also been reported at Kauśāṁbī. A copper amulet is known from Besanagar (*ARASI*, 1914-15: Pl.LV.41, 86). It is dated between CE 100-200. One of copper from Besanagar belongs to the Gupta period.

*Triratna*s are also known from Peḍḍabankur, Satanikoṭṭa, Dhulikaṭṭa, etc., in the south India. The range for this is confined to fifth century BC to third century CE. This roughly corresponds to the period of prosperity of Buddhism in India. It is quite striking that *triratna* as an object of jewellery has been depicted in a number of sculptures of the Early School of Indian Art (Barua 1979: Pl. LVX.82; Cunninghum 1966: Pl.L.3-6, Pl. XXI, 35-6).

The practice of wearing *triratna* amulets was very common. In the Alakanandā Yaksī's neck ornaments are seen two *triratna* (*fig.* 12.5) amulets (Barua 1979: Pl. LXVI.72). In the finest Śuṅga sculpture of Sirima Devata a similar ornament adorns her neck (Barua 1979: Pl. LXV.78). Two *triratna* amulets hang in the neck ornament of Siṁhika Yakṣiṇī (Barua 1979: Pl. LXIII.82). In the pillar at Batanmara *triratna* adorns the necklace (Cunningham 1966: Pl.L.3-6; Pl. XXI, 35-6). The Pitalkhora Yakṣa wears a necklace with two *triratna* (*fig.* 12.6) with grinning human faces (Deshpande 1959: Pl. LVI.81). Mehrauli Yakṣiṇī also wears two *triratnas* with human face. (Agarwala, 1965: 102-3) *Triratnas* are shown in the ornamental penals of the rail coping (Barua 1979: Pl. XXXVII.32). Bodhi tree is flanked by *triratnas* being worshipped (Barua 1979: Pl. XVII.13.a). Apart from its ornamental value it has been an object of worship from very early times. It profusely decorates every part of the pillars, gateways and also the sculptural themes themselves at the *stūpas* of Bhārhut, Sāñcī, Amarāvatī, western Indian caves, Nāgārjunikoṇḍa, Sārnāth, Mathurā, etc. The earliest sculptures at Bhārhut date to *c.* second century BC, later sculptures at Nāgārjunikoṇḍa belong to about the third century CE. But the material evidence goes back to the beginning days of Buddhism. At Taxilā, *triratna* amulets are known as early as the fourth century BC.

A female figure from Sārnāth ascribed to the Kuṣāṇa period (*ARASI*, 1907-8), also shows *triratna* amulet in her garland. Arch of eastern gateway is flanked by two *triratnas*. Relief of an upright showing representation of the worship of *vajrāsana*, flanked by two beautiful *triratnas* (Munshi 1957: Pl.14.a). Prasenjit pillar shows the worship of *triratna* with *vajrāsana* (Barret 1954: Pl. XX.65). Amarāvatī dome slab's top is flanked by three *triratnas* (Barret 1954: Pl. 20). *Buddhapada* is adorned by *triratna* on the palm (Sivaramamurti 1956: Pl.XXI.2, 20, 169). In *mahāparinirvāṇa* worship scene is flanked by rows of three *triratna* (Saraswati 1957: 44). In some stray sculptures at Amarāvatī datable to the third century CE worship of *triratna* is seen (Saraswati 1959: Pl. 13). Śākyas adoring Buddha at Kapilavastu and Amarāvatī *āyāgapaṭa* (Munshi 1957: Pl. 23a). Lion capital of the queen of *Rajubala*, Kuṣāṇa period shows *triratnas*.

Representations of *triratna*s are met with at the beginning of some inscriptions at Kudā, Mahād, Beḍsā, Junnar and Nāsik (Burgess 1964). A terracotta figurine from Pauni shows *triratna* in the centre (Deo and Dhavalikar 1968: fig. 27.7). The necklace of the lady from Pauni depicted in terracotta figure has three strings. The central pendant is in the shape of a *triratna* with the horns up (Deo 1972: fig. 7, 234) (*fig*. 12.7).

Miscellaneous

CYLINDRICAL AMULETS (TĀVEEZ)

These consist of cylindrical-shaped amulets having capped ends, with loops for threading. These are decorated with heart-shaped motif, dots and circles, beadings, parallel lines and flower designs.

Specimens are known from Koṇḍāpur and Taxilā, in glass, gold, silver and terracotta. Terracotta specimens are made from moulds. Gold and silver specimens are known from Taxilā (Beck 1941). These are attributed to *c*. 300-200 BC level. Another specimen from Sirkāp dated to *c*. CE 100 with two strings each for suspension and decorated with parallel circles round the centre of the amulet. Another one is a rare amulet of glass with bulging centre upon which is the perforation. At Koṇḍāpur (Dikshit 1954: Pl. V.148) cylindrical amulets bear bands or ribs over them. These were hang by the use of metal caps over them, above, which are loops fitted.

Specimens from Maharashtra are dated between 200 BC to CE 300 whereas outside Maharashtra it belongs to 300 BC to CE 100. It could possibly be an ear-ornament as seen depicted in the *yakṣa* figures at Bhārhut (Barua 1979).

A female figurine from Pauni made of terracotta wears cylindrical amulets held by gold catches at either end like the middle jewels in the Bharhut *stūpa* sculptures (Deo and Dhavalikar 1968: fig. 27.7). A *śālabhañjikā* in Mathura Museum (SO IV 27) wears a cylindrical amulet in her necklace (*fig*. 12.8).

These parallels from other sites and references in literature, sculptural depiction, showing typological similarities give some inclinations of contact and trade between these sites.

We find that in the early centuries of the Christian era the patterns divide themselves into cultural centres at many places. Some specimens from the adjoining areas in Maharashtra are lacking, except some sporadic one's on contact sites. In the Sātavāhana period a different picture of the bead industry emerges. This in Indo-Roman period reached at the zenith and as a result we find many new types.

Clay imitation of Roman coins makes appearance for the first time. The abundance of arika-nut shape beads also points to trade routes as its concentration is on trade-centres like Ter, Prakāshe, Brahmapurī, Arikāmeḍu, Nāsik, Nevāsā, etc.

Faience beads in India appear only after the beginning of the Christian era. Faience beads belonging to the Indo-Roman levels in Maharashtra have its counterpart in the same material from Charsada, Candravallī, Koṇḍāpur and Sirkāp. This points towards grand-trunk road.

Due to the impact of Indo-Roman trade we find glass appears to be used on a large scale. The beads with, yellow-matrix, gold foils are found in the early centuries of the Christian era mainly from trade emporiums like, Kolhāpur, Karāḍ, Paiṭhan, Ter, and Koṇḍāpur, i.e., the west-east route in south Maharashtra. Same is the case with small pillar-like (*fig*. 9.7) pendant of terracotta prepared out of double-mould. Exactly similar spacers are reported from Tripurī, Ujjain, Karāḍ, Kolhāpur, and Koṇḍāpur. These point towards the north-south route.

Roman contact is amply compensated by a large variety of types both hybrid and of foreign origin. Some of these unique specimens without any parallel in India are dumb-bell-shaped pendant made of copper from Nevāsā (*fig*. 9.8). The moulded chain bead of green glass from Nevāsā (*fig*. 9.10). The Nāga-hood bead thought similar to the *śrīvasta* motif in outline is distinctly a serpent bead, which depicts the vertebra minutely and clearly. The Chevron bead from Prakāshe (*fig*. 9.11). It is presumably copied from a metal prototype. The teeth of the chevron are so ingeniously fashioned as to dovetail into each other for the purpose of threading in a chain. Another unique specimen is the faggot bead made of terracotta from Ter (*fig.* 9.12).

It is quite possible that these specimens came from bead-making sites like Taxilā in the north and Koṇḍāpur in the south, etc., or from a foreign land, as we have not been able to establish a bead-making site in Maharashtra. Compare to other sites in India the data is negligible.

When we talk about Bull amulets all of them are made from clay moulds, indicating their use on a mass scale. The similarity of the depiction indicates its popular amuletic use in the early centuries of the Christian era.

An emerging aspect of the study of these small ornamental pieces clearly indicate that religious feelings were manifest in a number of ways, one of which was employed in carving or preparing them as symbols in decorative jewellery for adornment. This is the formative period during which the iconic development of image-sculptures were taking shape and in these amuletic pendants one can trace out the origin of various religious motifs and symbols. The symbols such as *pīpal* leaf, *śrīvatsa*, *makara*, *nandī*, *svastika* — all represents certain idea of motifs of supernatural importance and when worn in necklace, it becomes an everlasting belief on the part of the weaver to remember.

A comparative assessment of the typical pendants found elsewhere in western, nort-western India and Gangetic valley testifies to the homogeneous cultural milieu of the society during the early historic period. The geographical zone of the Mauryas and Sātavāhanas had a wide network of trade routes and it is no wonder that the pendants and amulets were extensively utilised in various towns and villages within the area especially in central India and northern Deccan. It also indicates the concentration at Kauṇḍinyapura, Brahmapurī and Paiṭhan with many varieties and in different material that it was a lapidary centre, where artisans manufactured on a vast scale for use. This is much true in cases where moulds were found in large numbers, especially made in terracotta. In other words, a study of amulets and pendants from Maharashtra reveal enough material for cross-cultural impact of various religious forces dominating the ancient Indian society during the early historic period.

Bibliography

Agrawala, V.S., *Handbook of Sculptures in the Curzon Museum of Archaeology*, Mathura, 1939.

———, *Studies in Indian Art*, Varanasi, 1965.

Agrawala, A., *Gupta Art*, Lucknow, 1947.

Agrawala, B., *Terracotta Figurines of Ahichhatra*, Lucknow, 1947.

———, *A Catalogue of Brāhmanical Images in Mathurā Art*, Lucknow, 1951.

———, *Harṣacarita —Eka Sāmskṛtika Adhyayana* (Hindi), Patna.

Allan, J., *Catalogue of the Coins of Ancient India*, London, 1936.

Altekar, A.S., V. Mishra, *Report on the Kumrahara Excavations* (*1951*-55), Patna, 1959.

Ansari, Z.D., M.S. Mate, *Excavation at Dwārka*, Pune, 1966.

Apte, V.M., *Social and Religious Life in the Gṛhya-sūtras*, Bombay, 1954.

Bachhofer, L., *Early Sculptures from Amarāvatī in British Museum*, London,1954.

Bali, S. (ed.), *Historical and Critical Studies in the Atharvaveda*, Delhi, 1981.

Bajpai, K.D., S.K. Pandey, *Malhār-1975-78*, Sagar, 1978.

Banerjea, J.N., *Development of Hindu Iconography*, Calcutta, 1956.

Banerjee, N.K., *Treasures of the National Museum*, New Delhi, 1992.

Banerjee, N.R., 'The Technique of the Manufacture of Stone Beads in Ancient Ujjain', *JAS*, 1.2, 1959.

Banerji, R.D., 'The Temple of Śiva at Bhumarā', *MASI*, 16, 1924.

Barrett, D., *Sculptures from Amarāvatī in the British Museum*, London, 1954.

Barua, B.M., *Gayā and Bodhagayā: Early History of the Holy lands*, Two Vols., Calcutta, 1934-7.

———, *Bhārhūt*, Parts 1-3, Patna, 1979.

Bateman, A.M., *Economic Mineral Deposits*, Bombay, 1950.

Beck, H.C., 'Classification and Nomenclature of Beads and Pendants', *Archaeologia* 77, Society of Antiquaries of London, 1929.

Beck, H.C., 'Beads from Taxila', *MASI* 65, Delhi, 1941.

Becker, E., *Escape from Evil*, New York.

Bhagwanlal, I., 'Antiquarian Remains at Sopārā and Padāna', *JBBRAS*, XV, 1885.

B.I.S.M., *Explorations at Karāḍ*, Bhāratīya Itihās Saṁśodhan Maṇḍal, Pune, 1949.

Bloomfield, M., *The Atharvaveda Encyclopedia of Indo-Aryan Research*, 2(1B), Bombay, 1899.

Brahmamuni, P., *Atharvavedīya Mantravidyā*, New Delhi, 1941.

Brown, J.C., 'India's Mineral Wealth', *India of Today*, Vol. 4, London, 1923.

Brown, P., *Indian Architecture: Hindu and Buddhist*, Bombay, 1965.

Budge, Sir. C.A., Wallis, *Encyclopaedia of Magic and Superstition*.

Burgess, J., *Buddhist Cave Temples and Their Inscriptions*, Varanasi, 1964.

Burgess, J., *The Buddhist Stūpas of Amarāvatī and Jaggeyyapeta*, Varanasi, 1970.

Chapekar, B.N., *Report on Excavation at Ter 1958*, Poona, 1969.

Clark, A., *Minerals*, Hamlyn, 1979.

Coomaraswamy, A.K., 'An Indian Crocodile', *BBMFA*, XXXIV.202 ,1936.

———, 'The Symbolism of the Dome', *IHQ*, XIV, 1938.

———, 'Ornament', *AB*, XXI, 1939.

———, *Yakṣas*, Part 1-2, New Delhi, 1980.

Cowell, F., *Jatakas*, Cambridge, 1907.

Cunningham, A., *Mahābodhī or the Buddhist Temple at Boddhagayā*, London, 1892.

———, *The Stūpa of Bhārhūt*, Varanasi, 1962.

———, *The Bhilsā Topes*, London, 1966.

Deglurkar, G.B., G. Lad, *Megalithic Raipur, 1985-90*, Pune, 1992.

Dehejiya, V., 'On modes of Visual Narration in Early Buddhist Art', *AB*, Sep. 1990.

Dept. of Archaeology, Maharashtra State, 1972. 'Ter Vastu Saṅgrahālayātila Purātan Vastūncha Parichaya', *BIS*, 9.33 -4.

Deo, S.B., *Mahārāshtrātila Utakhanane* (Marathi), Bombay, 1962.

———, 'A Note on Makarika Ornament', *JOI* , XVI.2, 1966.

———, *Ter* (Marathi), Bombay.

———, 'Coiffure, Dress and Ornaments of Pauni Sculptures', S.B. Deo, (ed.), *Seminar Papers and Archaeological Congress*, Nagpur, 1972.

———, *Indian Beads* (in press.)

———, Dhavalikar, *Paunār Excavation 1967*, Nagpur, 1968.

Deo, S.B., Gupte, *Excavations at Bhokardan*, Nagpur, 1973.

Deo, S.B., Joshi, *Pauni Excavation 1969-70*, Nagpur, 1972.

Deshpande, M.N., 'The Rock-cut Caves of Pitalkhora in the Deccan, *AI*, 15, 1959.

Dhavalikar, M.K., *Sāñcī: A Cultural Study*, Poona, 1965.

———, 'Eye-goddesses in India and their West Asian Parallels', *Anthropos*, 60, 1965.

———, 'Paiṭhan Terracottas', *JISOA*, VIII, 1975-6.

———, *Masterpieces of Indian Terracottas*, Bombay, 1977.

Dey and Brown, 1973, *India's Mineral Geology and Mineral Resources of Maharashtra*, Nagpur.

Dikshit, K.N., 'Buddhist Relics from Sopārā: Re-examined', *JGRS*, 1.4, 1939.

Dikshit, K.R., *Maharashtra in Maps*, Bombay, 1986.

Dikshit, M.G.,'Some Beads from Ahichhatrā', U.P., *AI*, 8, 1952.

———, 'Some Beads from Koṇḍāpur', *HAS*, 16, 1952.

———, 'Notes on Some Indian Amulets', *BPWM*, 2, 1954.

———, *Tripurī 1952*, Saugar, 1955.

———, *Excavations at Kauṇḍinyapura*, Bombay, 1968.

Directorate of Geology and Mining Geology and Mineral Resources of Maharashtra, Nagpur, 1968.

Fergusson, J., *History of Indian and Eastern Architecture*, London, 1891.

———, Burgess, J., *Cave Temples of India*, London, 1880.

Fleet, J.F., 'Tagara: Ter', *JRAS*, 1901.

Foucher, A., *The Beginnings of Buddhist Art*, London, 1977.

Francis, P., 'Indian Agate Beads', *The World of Beads Monograph Series*: 6, 1982.

Ganapati Sastri, T., *Kālidāsa's Kumārasambhava*, Bombay, 1916.

———, *Raghuvaṁśa*, Bombay, 1929.

Ganguli, K.K., 'Symbols in Early Indian Jewellary', *IHQ* 16, 1940.

Gazetteer of Bombay City and Island, Vol. 1, 1978.

Gaur, R.C., *Excavations at Atrañjikherā*, Delhi, 1983.

George, R.D., *Minerals and Rocks*, 1942.

Ghate, S.N., 'Late Quarternary Palaegeography of the Littoral Zone of North Koṅkaṇ, Maharashtra', PH.D. Thesis, University of Poona, 1975.

Ghosh, A., 'Sirkāp: 1944-45', *AI*, 4, 1947.

———, *An Encyclopedia of Indian Archaeology*, New Delhi, 1989.

Gupta, P.L., 'Coins from Brahmapurī Excavations', *BDCRI*, 21, 1963.

Gyani, R., 'Sopārāmā Purātattvanaveṣaṇa', *JGRS* 1.4, 1939.

Hallade, M., *The Gāndhāran Style*, London, 1968.

Handiqui, K.K., *Yaśastilaka and Indian Culture*, Solāpur, 1968.

Hargreaves, H., 'Excavations at Sārnāth', *AR-ASI*, 1914-15.

Inghot, *Gāndhāra Art in Pākistan*, New York, 1957.

———, Jaiminiya Upaniṣad Brāhmaṇa' *JAOS*, (1896): 16.1.

Jain, G., *Yaśastilaka kā Sāṁskṛtika Adhyayana* (Hindi), Amritsar, 1967.

Jain, J.C., *Life in Ancient India as Depicted in the Jaina Cannon*, Bombay, 1947.

Jamkhedkar, A.P., *Vāsudevahiṇḍi —A Cultural Study*, Delhi, 1984.

Joshi, M. (ed.)., *Bhāratīya Saṁskriti Kośa*, Part 4, Pune, 1967.

Joshi, N.P., *Mathurā Sculptures*, Mathura, 1966.

———, *Journal of Asiatic Society of Bengal*, LVII, 1888.

Karambelkar, V.W., *The Athrvavedic Civilization*, Nagpur, 1959.

Khandalwala, K., 'Brahmapurī — A Consideration of the Metal Objects Found in the Kundangār Hoard', *LK*, 7, 1960.

Kosambi, D.D., 1962, *Myth & Reality*, Bombay, 1962.

Kramrich, S., *India Sculpture*, London, 1933.

Krishna Deva, 'Excavations at Rājghāṭ, near Banaras', *ABIHI*, III, 1940.

———,V. Mishra, *Vaishali Excavations: 1950,* Vaishali, 1961.

Lal, B.B., 'Śiśupālgarh 1948: an Early Historical Fort in East India', *AI*, 5, 1949.

Longhurst, A.H., 'Pallava Architecture', *MASI*, 17, 1924.

———, 'Nāgārjunikoṇḍa', *MASI*, 54, 1939.

Macdonell, K., 'Vedic Index 2', *Man,* XXXII (33).

Mackay, E.J.H., *Further Excavations at Mohenjo-Daro*, New Delhi, 1938.

Margabandu, C., 'Some Amuletic Pendants of Central and Western India', *Archaeological Congress and Seminer Papers*, ed. S.B. Deo, Nagpur, 1972.

Marg Publications, *Symbols and Manifestations of Indian Art*, Bombay, 1984.

Marshall, J., 'Excavations at Sahet-Mahet', *AR ASI*, 1910-11.

———, 'Excavations at Bhita', *AR*, *ASI*, 1911-12.

———, *Mohenjo Daro and Indus Civilization*, London, 1931.

———, *Taxilā*, 3 Vols., Cambridge, 1951-3.

———, *A Guide to Sāñcī*, Delhi,1955.

———, *The Buddhist Art of Gāndhāra*, Cambridge, 1960.

———, *The Monuments of Sāñcī*, 3 Vols., Foucher 1983.

———, Konow, S., 'Excavations at Sārnāth', *AR ASI*, 1907-8.

———, (ed.), 'The Hymns of the Atharvaveda', (tr. M. Bloomfield) *SBE*, XLII, Oxford, 1897.

Max Müller (ed.), Vinaya Piṭaka, *SBE*, XVII, 1882.

Mehta, R.N., *Excavations at Timbervā*, Baroda, 1955.

———, *Excavation At Nagara*, Baroda, 1968.

———, *Excavation at Jokhā*, Baroda, 1971.

Mitra, D., *Buddhist Monuments*, Calcutta, 1971.

Mishra, V.N., V. Shinde, R.K. Mohanty, K. Dalal, A. Mishra, L. Pandey, and J. Kharakwal, 1995. 'The Excavations at Bālāthal: their Contribution to the Chalcolithic and Iron Age Cultures of Mewar, Rajasthan', *Man & Enviornment*, XX.1

Mode, H., Chandra, S., *Indian Folk Art*, Bombay, 1985.

Narain, A.K., T.N. Roy, *The Excavations at Prahlādpūr:1963*, 1968.

———, *Excavations at Rājghāṭ*, 1976.

Rao, S.R., 'Excavations at Amreli: A Kshatrapa-Gupta Town', *BMPG*, 18, 1966.

Rao, S.R., 'Excavation at Kānherī — 1969', *Studies in Indian History and Culture*, P. B. Desai Felicitation Volume, Dharwar, 1971.

Ray, N., *Mauryan and Śuṅga Art*, Calcutta, 1965.

Rosenfield, J., *The Dynastic Art of the Kuṣāṇas*, California, 1967.

Roy, T.N., 'A Note on Makara Figurines', *Puratattava*, 3, 1969.

Punyavijaya, Muni, (ed.), 1957, *Aṅga-vijjā*.

Puri, B.N., *Excavations at Rairh*, Jaipur.

Sahni, D.R. *Archaeological Remains and Excavations at Sāṁbar*, Jaipur.

———, *Excavations at Bairāt*, Jaipur.

Sankalia, H.D., S.B. Deo., *Report on the Excavation at Nāsik and Jorwe, 1950-51*, Poona, 1955.

Sankalia, H.D., M.G. Dikshit, *Excavation at Brahmapurī (Kolhāpur) 1954-6*, Poona, 1952.

Sankalia, H.D., B. Subbarao, S.B. Deo, *The Excavations at Maheśvar and Navdātoli: 1952 - 53*, Poona: Baroda, 1958.

———, *et al.*, *From History to Pre-history at Nevāsā, 1954-56*, Poona, 1960.

Saraswati, S.K., *A Survey of India Sculpture*, Calcutta, 1957.

Sastri, J.V.P., Rao, Kasturi Bai, 1984, *Veerapuram Excavation*, Hyderabad.

Schlingloff, D., *Studies in Ajantā Paintings*, Delhi, 1987.

Seligmann, *Heil und Schutzmittel*, Stuttgart, 1920.

Sharma, G.R., *The Excavations at Kauśāmbī: 1957-59*, Allahabad, 1960.

———, 'Excavations at Kauśāṁbī: 1949-50', *MASI*, 74, 1969.

Sharma, P. (ed.), *Caraka-Saṁhitā*, Vol. 2, Varanasi, 1983.

Sharma, R.C., *The Splendour of Mathurā Art and Museum*, Delhi, 1994.

Shende, N.J., 'Foundations of the Atharvanic Religion', *BDCRI*, IX, 1948.

Sinha, B.P., S.R. Roy, *Vaiśālī Excavations: 1958-62*, Patna, 1969.

Sinha, K.K., *Excavations at Śrāvastī — 1959*, Varanasi, 1967.

Singh, C. (ed.), *Pathways to Literature, Art and Archaeology*.

Sivaramamurti, C., 'Geographical and Chronological Factors in Indian Iconography', *AI*, 6, 1950.

———, 'Amrāvatī Sculptures in the Madras Govt. Museum', *BMGM*, (NS) 4, 1977.

Spence, L., *An Encyclopedia of Occultism*, Delhi, 1984.

Spooner, D.B., 'Excavations at Sahri-Bahlol', *ARASI*, 1909-10.

Subbarao, B., *Baroda Through the Ages*, Baroda, 1953.

Subrahmanyam, R., 'Nagajunikoṇḍa: 1954-60', *MASI*, 75, 1975.

Syed, Y., 'Paiṭhan Excavations', *ARADND*, 1936-37, 1936.

Thapar, B.K., 'Māskī 1954: a Chalcolithic Site of Southern Deccan', *AI*, 13, 1957.

———, 'Prakāshe 1955: A Chalcolithic Site in the Tapti Valley', *AI*, 20-21, 1967.

Wadia, D.N., *Geology of India*, London, 1944.

Wadia, M.D.N., *Minerals of India*, Delhi, 1966.

Wheeler, R.E.M., 'Brahmagiri and Chandravallī: 1947, Megalithic and other Cultures in the Mysore State', *AI*, 4, 1947.

Whitney, 'Athrvaveda Saṁhitā', *HOS*, 1905.

Yazdani, G., *Ajantā*, 4 Vol., London, 1931-55.

Young, G.M., 'A New-Hoard from Taxilā, (Bhir Mound)', *AI*, 1, 1946.

Vats, M.S., *Excavations at Harappā*, 2 Vols., Calcutta, 1940.

———, 'The Gupta Temple at Deogarh', *MASI*, 70, 1952.

Zim and Shaffer, *Rocks and Minerals*, New York, 1959.

Zimmer, H., *The Art of Indian Asia*, 2 Vols., ed. J. Compbell, New York.

Zimmer, H., *Myths and Symbols in Indian Art and Civilization*, Princeton, 1974.

Index